FORGOTTEN WARRIORS

HOUSTON STIFF **Routine Patrol**   1967, Oil on canvas, 39″ × 20″ (U.S. Marine Corps Art Coll.)

FORGOTTEN WARRIORS
COMBAT ART FROM VIETNAM

DENNIS L. NOBLE

PRAEGER

Westport, Connecticut
London

Copyright Acknowledgments

The author and publisher thank the following for allowing the use of their material:

Excerpts from *Dispatches* by Michael Herr, copyright (c) 1968, 1970, 1977 by Michael Herr; reprinted by permission of Alfred A. Knopf, Inc. and Picador as United Kingdom publisher.

Excerpts from "Cutters and Sampans" by Dennis Noble, reprinted from *Proceedings* with permission, copyright (c) 1984 U.S. Naval Institute.

Excerpts from "Perspectives" by Dennis Noble, in *Vietnam*, April 1991, reprinted by permission of Empire Press.

Library of Congress Cataloging-in-Publication Data

Noble, Dennis L.
    Forgotten warriors : combat art from Vietnam / Dennis L. Noble.
        p. cm.
    Includes bibliographical references (p.   ) and indexes.
    ISBN 0–275–93868–9 (alk. paper)
    1. Vietnamese Conflict, 1961–1975—Art and the conflict.   2. Art, American.   I. Title.
DS559.8.A78N63 1992
959.704′3373—dc20   91–44451

British Library Cataloguing in Publication Data is available.

Library of Congress Catalog Card Number: 91–44451
ISBN: 0–275–93868–9

First published in 1992

Praeger Publishers, 88 Post Road West, Westport, CT 06881
An imprint of Greenwood Publishing Group, Inc.

Printed in the United States of America

∞™

The paper used in this book complies with the Permanent Paper Standard issued by the National Information Standards Organization (Z39.48–1984).

10 9 8 7 6 5 4 3 2 1

For All Who Served in Vietnam and to All
Who Have Died in the "Undeclared Wars"

We had been told, on leaving our native soil, that we were going to defend the sacred rights conferred on us by so many of our citizens settled overseas, so many years of our presence, so many benefits brought by us to populations in need of our assistance and our civilization.

We were able to verify that all this was true, and, because it was true, we did not hesitate to shed our quota of blood, to sacrifice our youth and our hopes. We regretted nothing, but whereas we over here are inspired by this frame of mind, I am told that in Rome factions and conspiracies are rife, that treachery flourishes, and that many people in their uncertainty and confusion lend a ready ear to the dire temptations of relinquishment and vilify our action.

I cannot believe that all this is true and yet recent wars have shown how pernicious such a state of mind could be and to where it could lead.

Make haste to reassure me, I beg you, and tell me that our fellow-citizens understand us, support us and protect us as we ourselves are protecting the glory of the empire.

If it should be otherwise, if we should have to leave our bleached bones on these desert sands in vain, then beware of the anger of the Legions!

—Marcus Flavinius, Centurion
in the 2nd Cohort of the Augusta
Legion, to his cousin Tertullus in Rome

CONTENTS

CONTENTS

x

ILLUSTRATIONS

PREFACE

In 1969, while stationed in San Francisco, I observed a U.S. Marine in uniform spat upon and called a baby killer. I felt the incident to be typical of what military people endured during the Vietnam War because of a confused homefront. I also thought that I would like to do something that would inform the public of what that unknown marine, and all the others who served during the long war, had to go through when they returned to the United States. Twelve years later, in 1981, while researching in the U.S. Marine Corps Historical Center, I came upon the opportunity to realize this goal. Noticing that the center contained an art collection, I sought out the curator, John T. Dyer, Jr., and inquired about the holdings of his department. I was intrigued to learn of the large amount of art held by the corps. The collection dealing with the Vietnam War, for example, ran to over 4,000 pieces of art. Curious, I began to peruse the works. After viewing Henry C. Casselli, Jr.'s *Corpsman* (Illus. 89), I was moved by the work enough to make me want to use the art of the Vietnam War in some manner. I then visited the art collections of the other branches of the armed forces, located in Washington, D.C. I found that, in general, the various artists had great sympathy for the men in the field, the "grunts," to use the vernacular of the Vietnam era. After completing my visits and upon further reflection, I felt that the combat art of the U.S. military offered a richer visual alternative to television and Hollywood in understanding the world of the combat soldier. The works would also offer the general public a chance to understand what service people in Vietnam endured, only to be shunned when they returned home.

It is more than likely that most Americans have obtained their perceptions of the Vietnam War through weekly television series and movies, closely followed by novels about the war. This is understandable, for to grasp the Vietnam War really requires a great deal of study. Furthermore, to pursue the reasons behind the many decision-making processes and operations, one must delve into archival holdings, many of which are still classified. It takes little effort to spend a few hours in a theater and be entertained and impressed by the visual effects of Hollywood. It is easy for the average citizen of today to succumb to the hyperbole of the public relations agent who claims that the latest film epic of Hollywood *really* shows the war.

I believe that through the influence of television we are a visually oriented society. This leads to the question: Do television and Hollywood give an accurate picture of the Vietnam War? Most important, do films show the world of the combat soldier? The purpose of this book is to use the combat art of the Vietnam War to provide a better visual method of understanding the world of the soldier in Southeast Asia.

As mentioned, this book is about how artists viewed the combat soldier. I believe it is important to focus on the man in the field, for he bore the brunt of the war and was the subject of the most misunderstanding on the homefront. While the focus is on that soldier, the narrative and the art will also depict some of the activities of the U.S. naval, air, and rear echelon forces in Southeast Asia. I have chosen to show a range of the activities of all of the armed forces in order to make the work representative of those who served. After all, sailors and airmen died in Vietnam, and there were many cases of attacks in the rear echelon, an area traditionally considered "safe." Space, however, prohibits the representation of every duty. Furthermore, the artists themselves did not portray every activity.

It is not the purpose of this book to argue whether the United States was right or wrong in its long involvement in Vietnam. Nor does it attempt to provide a new and insightful text on the war. The art will speak for itself, and the narrative will be used to complement the art or to explain certain aspects of the war that the artists were depicting. Just as combat art can be used to provide a better visual image of the Vietnam War, so can literature help in understanding how some soldiers, sailors, airmen, and marines felt about their experiences. Whenever possible, the men will be allowed to speak for themselves, through oral histories and letters sent home. Some of the narrative contains excerpts from a few of the hundreds of novels that have appeared about the American experience in Southeast Asia, while other passages are from official histories. For example, the quote from Michael Herr's work describing a night patrol, in chapter 5, nicely complements the works by Walter Giordano and others that follow it. In other words, the reader should not expect this to be a history of the Vietnam War. Rather, it is about how a group of artists felt about the men who bore the brunt of the war and, whenever possible, how the actual soldiers, sailors, airmen, and marines felt about their experiences. The detailing of the war, its battles, and its consequences are best left to scholarly works. My purpose is to use art and literature to provide a view of the forgotten men who fought in Southeast Asia and who are all too often overlooked in the histories of war.

Another aspect of this work developed because a few combat artists examined some of the little-known activities of the forgotten warriors. Noel Daggett's works on the U.S. Coast Guard, for example, made it necessary to explain why the U.S. Coast Guard was in Vietnam. A good spin-off of these explanations is that the men who did not receive the recognition for their roles can, belatedly, be brought to the attention of the general public.

A definition of combat art and an explanation of the methods used in selecting illustrations for this work are needed. For the purposes of this book, combat art is defined as those works produced during the war years by artists who were actually in Vietnam, and which are now held by the various branches of the U.S. military. Other artists served in Vietnam in the rank and file but did not serve as official combat artists. These artists produced, and continue to produce, works about their experiences or views of the conflict. Much of this art is, however, difficult to track, so I concentrated my research on works most readily available to the general public, those held by the American military. This in no way implies that any other art on the war is unacceptable.

With thousands of pieces of art to select from, my task was difficult in the extreme. The criteria for inclusion in this work were: Does the art depict the world of the combat soldier? Does the art, especially for chapters 7 and 8, accurately depict some aspect of the country and people of South Vietnam and something of the air and sea wars? In general, I wanted to use the sensitivity of the artist to express the emotions of war, not to record historical events, although the origin of many works can be pinpointed. For example, the drawing by A. Michael Leahy entitled *Close Air for INDIA* (Illus. 75), in chapter 5, gives information on the event recorded and even the people, one of whom was the son-in-law of President Lyndon Johnson.

Nor should the reader expect this book simply to illustrate a narrative of the war. Rather, the illustrations best symbolize what the artist was trying to convey on a given topic. John O. Wehrle's *Landing Zone* (Illus. 11), for instance, shows the loneliness of the infantryman in combat. In short, we will not see exactly what happened at 0600, November 25, 1969, at Ca Mau. What will be presented is how the artist felt about what he observed at Ca Mau. I alone am responsible for the selection. Space prevents the reproduction of all the combat art, and many interesting and very good pieces had to be omitted.

This book is meant for the general reader who wishes to have a better visual understanding of the Vietnam War and those who most actively fought it, not for the art historian or the art critic. Therefore, there is very little discussion of painting techniques and materials. Again, because this work is for the general reader, a discussion of which of the people included within are "pure" artists and which are illustrators is not included. For the purposes of this book, all those whose works are presented within will be called artists. In the same vein, the ranks of the military artists are not given, allowing the reader to judge the works on their merits alone, not on the rank of the artists. All the art appears here in black and white. I believe the works are so powerful that the art does not suffer when reproduced in this manner.

All the works reproduced here, with two exceptions, were completed during the American involvement in Vietnam. The two works by Keith Ferris, in chapter 7, are so well researched and so well represent the air war in Vietnam that I have included them in this book.

With the main focus of this work on the way artists viewed the combat soldier in the Vietnam War, chapters 1 through 6 deal with different aspects of the grunt's world: patrols, periods in the rear, fighting the terrain and weather, and the effects of combat and its aftermath. Chapter 7 deals with the machinery of war. Chapter 8 gives the reader an overview of how some artists and writers viewed the country and people of South Vietnam. The importance of movies, television series, and novels on the war has been mentioned. So that the reader may have a grasp of some of the better movies and novels on Vietnam in order to compare them with the art contained in this book, William J. Palmer of Purdue University, a recognized authority on the films and novels of the war, provides an essay on the subject.

The views contained within the main portion of this book are mine and those in the appendix are of Professor Palmer.

Finally, were I idealistic, I would like to think that perhaps the observations and art of this work would cause those that are in a position to send troops to far-off places to pause and reflect on just what they are committing young people to endure. Most important, I would like to think that the book would make those who actually have to undergo combat reflect before rushing headlong into battle. I am, however, realistic enough to know that this will probably never happen. Even as these words are being written (December 1991), there has been another undeclared war, albeit a short one that seems to have made Americans proud. It is my hope that, at the least, this work may help those of other generations to understand a generation that fought a war and endured the hardships of that conflict as well as any force in history, only to be shunned and forgotten in their time.

ACKNOWLEDGMENTS

During the course of preparing this book, it has been my good fortune to meet a group of people who are some of the most dedicated keepers of special collections in the Washington, D.C., area. Indeed, all the curators of the various military art collections went above and beyond the call of duty in providing me with information and reproductions from their holdings.

At the U.S. Army Center of Military History, Marylou Gjernes provided a great deal of her valuable time in searching for needed photographs. Alice Price at the U.S. Air Force Art Collection provided a great deal of information and was always ready for the necessary follow-up questions. Jim Ward and Virginia Donnelley of the U.S. Coast Guard's Community Relations Division helped a great deal. John D. Barnett of the U.S. Navy's Combat Art Collection went out of his way to provide me with materials very quickly and efficiently; while Addie Wimbush of the Navy Combat Art Center even took my rough handwritten source notes and placed them in meaningful order. Thank you.

From the above, I hope it is clear that all of the curators of the military art collections were helpful. I would, however, especially like to thank John T. Dyer, Jr., of the U.S. Marine Corps' Art Collection. Mr. Dyer spent an entire week with me explaining the art program of the Corps and, over the years, has given me a great deal of information and encouragement on this project. A combat artist himself, Mr. Dyer's works appear throughout this book. To say thank you somehow seems inadequate for all the help he provided me.

William J. Palmer of the Department of English, Purdue University, allowed me to gain an insight into the better lit-

ACKNOWLEDGMENTS

erature and films of the Vietnam War. He consistently encouraged me to continue with this project. Professor Palmer took time out from his demanding writing and teaching schedule to write an essay on the films and literature of the war for this work.

Trella Koczwara, one of the two women combat artists of the Vietnam War, graciously took the time to respond to a questionnaire on her experiences during the war. Her insights will allow readers to better understand the work of the combat artists in Vietnam.

Mildred Vasan has proved to be an understanding and helpful editor. Penny Sippel and Barbara Goodhouse helped to guide the manuscript through production.

Bernard C. Nalty, of the Office of Air Force History, Washington, D.C., provided me with material on that service's efforts in Vietnam.

Peggy Brady, of Port Angeles, Washington, did her usual excellent job of locating inconsistencies and errors in spelling. Greg Shield and Colleen Cunningham, also of Port Angeles, Washington, took time from their busy schedules to read and critique the manuscript. I thank them for their efforts. Earl Hess, of Lincoln Memorial University, read and offered comments during the first stages of the manuscript.

Lloyd and Jamye Wisecup of the Bay Motel at Clallam Bay, Washington, provided me with the ideal location to write.

Where this work has merit, it is because of the help and encouragement given to me by all of the above-named people. I am, of course, responsible for both selection of the art and content.

xxiv

ABBREVIATIONS

MILITARY RANKS

Adm.	Admiral
Capt.	Captain
Cmdr.	Commander
Col.	Colonel
Corp.	Corporal
Gen.	General
Lcpl.	Lance Corporal
Lt.	Lieutenant
lLT	First Lieutenant
Lt. Cmdr.	Lieutenant Commander
Lt. Col.	Lieutenant Colonel
Pfc.	Private First Class
Pvt.	Private
Sfc.	Sergeant First Class
Sgt.	Sergeant
SP	Specialist
Ssgt.	Staff Sergeant

MILITARY TERMS

AEF	American Expeditionary Force
APC	armored personnel carriers
ASPB	assault support patrol boat
ATC	armored troop carriers
CAC	Combat Artist Corps

CCB	command communication boat
CIB	Combat Information Bureau
CIDG	Civilian Irregular Defense Group
DMZ	Demilitarized Zone
LAW	light assault weapon
LCM	landing craft, medium
LCVP	landing craft, vehicle, personnel
LST	landing ship, tank
LZ	landing zone
NVA	North Vietnamese Army
PBR	patrol boat, river
PCF	patrol craft, fast
POW	prisoner of war
RAG	River Assault Group
SEAL	Sea, Air, Land
VC	Viet Cong

Introduction

THE FORGOTTEN
WARRIORS

Gallons of ink were spilled and voices raised, in reason and in anger, during the United States' long war in Vietnam. Arguments centered on the legality, the illegality, the morality and immorality of the conflict. Did the United States have the right to interfere in another country's civil war? Was this a civil war or was it another example of the encroachment of Godless Communism? Demonstrations against the war seemed to appear almost nightly on the evening television news, while the average person in the street seemed willing to discuss the domino theory or variations on the same theme. Forgotten amid all of this rhetoric were the men and women who actually served in Vietnam. As symbols of an unpopular war, a confused homefront seemed willing either to forget them completely or to picture anyone returning from Southeast Asia as a mindless killer. " 'What was it like over there?' we were asked from the moment we got off the Freedom Bird. And then: 'Did you kill anyone?' "[1]

Some servicemen and women faced angry epithets and physical abuse. Perhaps worse than the physical or verbal abuse was the veteran's perception of an attempt on the part of the general public completely to shunt from its consciousness anyone returning from Southeast Asia. This perception seems valid. Throughout the long war, even when the United States had over 500,000 troops in South Vietnam and a military draft that could provide more, there were no weekly television programs, no Hollywood epics, and very few novels that gave the general public a personal view of the Vietnam experience; perhaps under the mistaken belief that if servicemen and women, as visual symbols of the war, were out of sight, the war could be put out of mind. (The only movie to be produced on the war during the long period of active American involvement in Southeast Asia was *The Green Berets*.) More charitably, perhaps the uniforms were a painful reminder of a confusing war.

In the late 1970s, public opinion on the Vietnam War shifted. Hollywood "discovered" the war. In 1978, for example, two productions dealing in some respect with the war in Vietnam won Academy Awards—*Coming Home* and *The Deer Hunter*. Since that date, there has been an almost steady stream of cinematic renditions, of varying quality, on the war. College students, instead of protesting the war, now insisted that courses be offered on Vietnam, and professors found the classes overflowing. In 1987, for example, Purdue University's Department of History offered a course on the Vietnam War and over the next two years had the highest amount of students enrolled at the junior level. The course began with 214 students enrolled, and for the next two years enrollment was at 216 and 217. Compare these figures to the enrollments in other junior-level history courses over the same period. The average number of students enrolled in 1987, for example, was 23, with the highest enrollment after the Vietnam War course at 107.[2]

Television began to offer programs that featured the military. Even commercials began using actors in military garb, touting everything from telephone service to sleeping tablets. By the 1980s, a weekly series that dealt with the war, or people serving in Vietnam, was on the small screen. Unlike the 1960s, however, when the intense debates on Southeast Asia centered on policy, Americans now wanted to know how the men and women who served in Vietnam had lived and survived. By the beginning of the 1990s, what had begun as a trickle of a few movies and television programs became a veritable flood. Nowhere is this more evident than in the number of novels appearing on the war. For example, one regional library network, the Western Library Network, registers some 443 novels on the Vietnam War, and this in no way covers all the works on the subject.[3]

Does the present flood of information on the Vietnam War mean that Americans can now understand the world of the combat soldier in Southeast Asia? In my opinion, the response to this question is a qualified no. The major problem in understanding what people endured in Vietnam is as old as war itself: How can anyone picture combat unless they have been in battle? Furthermore, the key to my response centers on Hollywood and to some extent on novels. Does Hollywood produce films that show the reality of combat, or does cinema, in fact, cause impressionable young men and women to think that war is a glorious test of bravery? While Robert Brent Toplin has argued quite cogently that moviegoers are adopting a "more reflective attitude toward war" and "are less tolerant than in earlier years of the gung ho approach to combat," it is my belief that this is true only for those that are insightful.[4]

Education, however, does not always provide this insight. I recall a graduate student's remark upon viewing the scene in *Apocalypse Now* where helicopters are attacking a village: "I'll bet it would be fun flying one of those!" Is this the message Francis Ford Coppola wanted audiences to receive? How then may we obtain a more accurate visual image of the war? The historian Arthur Marwick notes that art and literature can be a "mirror of the age" in which they are produced.[5] If Marwick is correct, then art by those who have witnessed combat, combined with the literature of those who witnessed war, may be one method of understanding the world of the combat soldier. Unbeknownst to most Americans, the U.S. military sent artists to record the Vietnam War. This little-known art form, called combat art by the military, may thus provide us with a better understanding of what people endured in Vietnam.

The combat photography of David Douglas Duncan and others raises the question, Why do we need art in this age of cameras and television? James Jones, in his work on the combat art of World War II, writes that almost all art produced for the government is "by definition propaganda." Jones noted that most governments do not wish the homefront to know the bad aspects of war and generally use art to make their actions acceptable to the public. All of this is correct, but as Jones then admits, "every now and then . . . one sees a given artist, as though pressed beyond his official commitment by his own emotions, suddenly breaking out from this more or less stated conspiracy . . . and then the works can rise to the level of greatness in art, which in the end can probably be defined simplistically as telling the whole truth beautifully, to create catharsis."[6]

The British artist Sir William Orpen once remarked that anyone could paint the 1917 trenches of the Somme, "but one could not paint the smell." No artist, or for that matter no photographer, can cross this barrier in war. Edgar M. Howell has succinctly pointed out that whether an artist can match the objectivity or the historical documentation of the camera in order to produce a "true" picture of war is a moot question. Is the artist trying to create a historical document? "Does he have to create 'war art'? Or is he, rather than defining a form, really attempting to symbolize or create a graphic expression of an idea, or make a statement of a mood? . . . Is not war simply what the men who make war see and feel? And is not true 'war art' simply what people feel when they view it, and the mental pictures it engenders?"[7] The combat artist of the Vietnam War brings an emotion to the work that expresses a mood that will trigger a reaction in the viewer. Having examined thousands of pieces of combat art on the conflict in Southeast Asia, I believe that the soldier in the field (the "bush") most engaged the sympathy of the majority of the artists. Henry C. Casselli, Jr., one of the best of the combat artists of the war, once remarked: "I had no idea of the horror that existed there. . . . I learned how to cry out there, how to hurt. I learned how to express my feelings. I was fortunate— I had a piece of paper on which to put it down."[8] Casselli's feelings are graphically transmitted most strongly in his works on marines in the field, and provide powerful visual statements on the compassion of men in a combat zone. In the final analysis, combat art can help provide contemporary Americans with the visual means of understanding those that served in the Vietnam War.

Visual methods of studying the Vietnam War are important. Television has made most Americans part of a visual society, and many have had their views on the war in Southeast Asia shaped by television or the movies. Indeed, television news coverage caused the war to be called America's first "living room" war, or a television war. Moreover, the Vietnam War itself has left us with a number of visual images that even contemporary Americans, or those of the 1960s who did not participate in the conflict, can readily identify with the war. A "Huey" helicopter, a child running down a road with her body showing burns from napalm bombs, the photograph of Col. Nguyen Ngoc Loan, South Vietnam's police chief, summarily executing a Viet Cong suspect with a pistol shot to the head, all seem to shout "Vietnam!" It is important, then, to provide visually oriented Americans who wish to understand what people endured in Vietnam with as many quality images as possible. The combat art of the Vietnam War offers one of the best means of obtaining this insight.

Although combat art covers the entire sweep of the Vietnam War, there are three special areas, all of which deal with the world of the combat soldier, where the artists of the war rise to great heights: the portrayal of the effects of prolonged exposure to the rigors of the bush on a soldier; the depiction of the effects of combat on the grunts; and the sense of comradeship among the infantrymen in the field.

Today's readers must realize that those who served in combat in Vietnam faced death or painful wounds, as have all combat soldiers, but they faced them feeling that no one cared about the soldiers themselves. Staff Sergeant Joseph Frederick Gilliand, in James Webb's novel *Fields of Fire*, best sums up how some Vietnam grunts perceived what the civilian world felt about them:

It ain't what happens here that's important. It's what's happening back *there*. Shit, . . . you'd hardly know there was a war on. It's in the papers, and college kids run around screaming about it instead of doing panty raids or whatever they were running around doing before, but that's it. . . . It's like nothing's really happened, except to other people. It isn't *touching* anybody.

We been abandoned. . . . We been kicked off the edge of the goddamn cliff. They don't know how to fight it, and they don't know how to stop fighting it. And back home it's too complicated, so they forget about it and do their rooting at football games.[9]

Thus, combat soldiers faced not only fear and anxiety in the bush, but also the mental anguish of verbal, and sometimes physical, abuse upon their return home. It is no wonder that many returning veterans have suffered psychological damage. I do not, however, wish to make these men into saints. The problem with any generalization, and especially one that deals with the Vietnam War, is that one can always find exceptions. At the height of the war, for example, the media made much of dissatisfaction among the troops, broadly hinting that all units had discipline problems and that some were on the verge of mutiny. Reports of "fraggings" (the killing of an unpopular leader by his own men, usually with a hand grenade) circulated freely. There is no doubt that some units were poorly led and had discipline problems. There were, however, those who wrote to their friends that they were "real proud" of their outfits; one army ranger even wrote that men in his company had "gone on patrols with broken ankles in order not to let their buddies down."[10] There were men who saw no reason why they should serve in Vietnam. Other men saw their tour of duty differently. One marine wrote to his family:

I don't like being over here, but I am doing a job that must be done—I am fighting an *inevitable* enemy that must be fought—now or later. . . . I am fighting to protect and maintain what I believe in and what I want to live in—a democratic society. If I am killed while carrying out this mission I want no one to cry or mourn for me. I want people to hold their heads high and be proud for me for the job I did.[11] (Emphasis in original)

Some men used drugs, others refused even to smoke cigarettes. Some soldiers seemed to enjoy combat, while others still have recurring nightmares. Some men committed crimes, others performed humanitarian acts. In short, the people who served in Vietnam were a slice of humanity caught up in something that they had very little say about, and to depict them as romantics, saints, or barbarians is not accurate or fair to them.

Many of the accounts contained within this book show that American troops won engagements or performed well in combat. This may cause some confusion among readers who have not studied the war in depth. A myth has grown up that Americans did poorly in combat. Much of that myth can be attributed to perceptions received from the media. Since the end of the conflict in Vietnam, newspapers, television, pundits, and others have produced a constant stream of information focusing on a recurring theme: The Vietnam War was the first war that America lost. Generally, anything that deals with the conflict has "lost" somewhere in the title, text, or subtext. This constant barrage has led many to believe that everything the United States did in South Vietnam was a failure, including the battles fought against the Viet Cong or North Vietnamese regulars. After all, didn't we lose? Yet, if one critically examines the record, this is simply not the case. American troops fought as well as in any war. I do not wish to go on record as saying we did not lose the war; however, in general, the U.S. military combat forces in the Vietnam War performed well and did win battles. In fact, most major engagements were won by American forces. It is also a fact that they lost some battles. Bear in mind that many of the fiction and nonfiction descriptions of combat included in this book are the observations of direct participants, which tend to be extremely personal. The narrators saw only their small part of the "big picture," and in many cases what they saw as a loss could well have been a victory. Nor do I wish the reader to feel the narrative proves that the U.S. military may have won the war if left alone to fight it without interference from politicians. Col. Harry G. Summers, Jr., one of the leading authorities on the Vietnam War, remarked in an interview with a North Vietnamese colonel, "You know you never defeated us on the battlefield." The Vietnamese officer replied: "That may be so. But it is also irrelevant."[12] Thus, the narrative can show victories without implying that the United States won the war.

By using combat art and concentrating on the men in the field, I hope to show what these forgotten warriors endured without romanticizing them. David Douglas Duncan, in his work on another group of forgotten warriors, the Korean War veterans, best sums up what this book is intended to convey.

I wanted to show the comradeship that binds men together when they are fighting a common peril. I wanted to show the way men live, and die, when they know that Death is among them, and yet they still find the strength to crawl forward armed only with bayonets to stop the advance of men they have never seen, with whom they have no immediate quarrel, men who will kill them on sight if given first chance. I wanted to show the agony, the suffering, the terrible confusion, the heroism which is everyday currency among those who actually pull the triggers of rifles aimed at other men known as "the enemy." I wanted to tell a story of war, as war has always been for men. Only their weapons, the terrain, the causes have changed.[13]

The common thread throughout the first six chapters of this book may be described very simply: the sensitivity of artists to show endurance, survival, the sense of caring for one's comrade, and the almost unbearable weight of combat upon very young men. There is also a background theme, caught in some of the better works, of a sense of helplessness, of being completely forgotten. The best works in this book are those that show the spark of human spirit in situations where humanity is usually lost.

NOTES

1. Quoted in Richard W. Grefrath, "Everyday Was Summertime in Vietnam: An Annotated Bibliography of the Best Personal Narratives," *Reference Services Review* 8 (October-December 1980): 23.

2. Letter, Professor Gordon R. Mork, Department of History, Purdue University, to Dennis L. Noble, August 10, 1990.

3. Printout, Western Library Network, Subject Headings, April 3, 1990. See also John Newman, *Vietnam War Literature: An Annotated Bibliography of Imaginative Works About Americans Fighting in Vietnam* (Metuchen, N.J.: Scarecrow Press, 1982).

4. Robert Brent Toplin, "Television's Civil War," *Perspectives: American Historical Association Newsletter* 28, no. 6 (September 1990): 22.

5. Arthur Marwick, *The Nature of History* (New York: Alfred A. Knopf, 1971), 183.

6. James Jones, *WW II* (New York: Grossett and Dunlap, 1975), 16.

7. Quoted in Edgar M. Howell, "An Artist Goes to War: Harvey Dunn and the A.E.F. War Art Program," *Smithsonian Journal of History* 2, no. 4 (Winter 1967–1968): 46.

8. John R. Kemp, "Henry Casselli," *American Artist* 51 (August 1987): 51–52.

9. James Webb, *Fields of Fire* (Englewood Cliffs, N.J.: Prentice-Hall, 1978), 175.

10. The letters were written by SP4 George T. Olsen, a ranger with Company G, 75th Infantry. He was killed in action on March 3, 1970. He

was twenty-three years old. Bernard Edelman, ed., *Dear America: Letters Home from Vietnam* (New York: Bantam Books, 1985), 43, 44, 50.

11. The letter was written by Pfc. Richard E. Marks, Company C, 3rd Marine Division. Two months after writing this letter he was killed. He was nineteen years old. Edelman, *Dear America*, 123, 124.

12. Quoted in Harry G. Summers, Jr., "The Bitter Triumph of Ia Drang," *American Heritage* 35, no. 2 (February/March 1984): 57.

13. David Douglas Duncan, *This Is War! A Photo-Narrative in Three Parts* (New York: Harper and Brothers, 1951), vi.

Chapter 1

PATROL

The war was fought in jungles, in elephant grass, in mountains, rice paddies, and open countryside. Many combat artists went into the bush with the troops and captured the various types of terrain in which patrols were conducted. The artists also captured something else that civilians may not realize about combat: the loneliness of the infantryman, even when surrounded by his fellow soldiers. James A. Fairfax's *Pointman* (Illus. 12) and John O. Wehrle's *Landing Zone* (Illus. 11) best capture the complete and utter isolation a soldier can feel in a war.

The image most Americans carry of the combat soldier in Vietnam comes largely from television news cameras: A small column of soldiers hacking their way through thick jungle foliage. Suddenly, the film becomes jumpy as sharp reports of automatic rifle fire from an ambush are heard. The camera, now held at ground level, pans to infantrymen lying flat, returning fire, or crouching and running to a better firing position. A radio crackles in the background, and shortly viewers see a jet dropping bombs or a helicopter gunship firing at the unseen enemy. The men then regroup and continue on, without ever seeing the enemy. Very few, if any, of Hollywood's epics on the war do anything to disabuse the general public of this image. In truth, a great deal of combat took place in the jungle and was at the company level. One can hardly fault the movies for stressing this type of warfare. The scenes of combat in the tropical forest give the viewer an eerie, almost primordial feeling. To walk the trails meant the real chance of danger. Tim O'Brien has graphically described how one soldier viewed the trails in *Going After Cacciato*:

The trails, like the land, were red. They were narrow. They were often dark, or shaded, and they mostly wound through the low places, following the contours of the land, and for this reason they sometimes flooded out during the rainy season. They were dangerous. No one was ever killed by a land mine or booby trap unless it was along a trail. Exposed, always watched, the trails were the obvious spots for ambush. Still, there were times when it was better to face the wet of a paddy or the itch of deep bush. There were times when a fast march along a trail, however perilous, was preferable to a slow march through hostile country. There were times when a mission required the use of trails. And there were times when it simply stopped mattering.[1]

Patrols making their way through tall, thick elephant grass faced the same problems as those in the forests. One army ranger wrote: "Try to imagine grass 8 to 15 feet high so thick as to cut visibility to one yard. . . . Then try to imagine walking through it while all around you are men possessing the latest automatic weapons who desperately want to kill you. You'd be amazed at how much a man can age on one patrol."[2]

The image of small company-sized engagements in difficult terrain is correct, up to a point. Small patrols and engagements, however, could lead to much larger battles. On October 19, 1965, for example, North Vietnamese regulars

1. THEODORE J. ABRAHAM
Reconnaissance Group Near Jackson Hole 1967, Pastel on paper, 19″ × 25″ (U.S. Army Center of Military Hist.)

attacked a small Special Forces camp at Plei Me, near the
Cambodian border. This was the opening salvo in what has
become known as the Battle of the Ia Drang Valley, or the
Ia Drang campaign. In a month of bitter fighting, large numbers of U.S. soldiers fought head-to-head with battalions of
North Vietnamese regulars. The U.S. Army's new concept of
airmobility—deploying troops rapidly by helicopter—was severely tested as the 1st Cavalry Division met strong resistance
by dedicated troops of the North Vietnamese Army (NVA).

After the attack on Plei Me began, intelligence sources
estimated that at least two NVA regiments, spearheaded by
Viet Cong (VC) shock troops, were determined to overrun the
camp, which would place them in an excellent position to
attack Pleiku, an area the 1st Cavalry Division had been sent
to Vietnam to protect.

Once the siege of the camp had been lifted, Gen. William
C. Westmoreland felt that the NVA troops threatened South
Vietnam's central region. He now decided that the division

PATROL

2. GARRY W. MOSS
Flanker 1970, Watercolor,
(U.S. Marine Corps Art
Coll.)

"must now do more than merely contain the enemy; he must be sought out aggressively and destroyed."[3] The campaign went under a number of code names: Long Reach, Silver Bayonet, and Green House. The 1st Brigade, made up of four infantry battalions, one light artillery battalion, and one aerial rocket artillery battery of gunship helicopters, began to seek out their enemy. Waiting for them were NVA regulars armed mostly with minimal equipment and sidearms.

Resistance was slight at first but began to stiffen as the campaign pushed deeper westward from Plei Me into the Ia Drang Valley. The use of helicopters and massive firepower seemed to be devastating the enemy, but some noticed that in the dense forest "the explosions and bullets seemed only to be tearing off tree limbs and killing a few clusters of men."[4] To move the soldiers rapidly throughout the area, a number of Landing Zones (LZs) were hacked out of the foliage, and the region was to be dotted with at least nine locations to land the helicopters. By November 9, the region west of Plei Me was considered clear of enemy troops. Col. Thomas W. Brown, however, believed that the NVA were still concentrating along the western Cambodian border. Colonel Brown

3. ROGER BLUM
Patrol in a Rice Paddy, Vietnam 1967, Watercolor on paper, 9⅞″ × 13⅞″ (U.S. Army Center of Military Hist.)

12

decided to reinvestigate the heavily jungled Ia Drang Valley
and later stated that "having drawn a blank up to this point,
I wasn't sure what we would find or even if we'd even find
anything."[5] What happened next became the most fearful
battle of the entire campaign and centered around LZ X-Ray.

Lt. Col. Harold G. Moore's 1st Battalion of the 7th Cavalry
began to probe the valley near the Chu Pong mountains.
Moore, suspecting trouble, wanted to airlift his initial company to consolidate an LZ in order to have the entire battalion
rapidly deployed and secure. He needed a space that would
be able to accommodate ten helicopters at once. Only two
fields of that size existed in the heavily forested area. He
chose a grassy field, designated LZ X-Ray, located near Chu
Pong, and ordered artillery fire to commence "softening up"
the field in preparation for an air assault. Helicopter gunships
made rocket and machine-gun attacks just prior to the first
Huey helicopters touching down. Unfortunately for Lieutenant Colonel Moore's battalion, LZ X-Ray was located near

4. HENRY C.
CASSELLI, JR.
Crossing the Rice Paddies
1968, Mixed media,
30″ × 40″ (U.S. Marine
Corps Art Coll.)

the mountain staging area of the decimated battalion-sized 33rd and three battalions of the 66th NVA Regiment. Nearby were three battalions of the 32nd. Moore's 20 officers and 411 men were facing some 2,700 NVA regular troops.[6]

Company B air assaulted into LZ X-Ray at 10:30 A.M. on November 14, 1965. The LZ contained thick elephant grass growing up to five feet in height, and the ground was dotted with eight-foot-high anthills. Moore, meeting no resistance, ordered the rest of the battalion into the LZ. At 12:45 P.M., Company B ran headlong into two companies of NVA infantrymen. Mortars and rockets began to hit the LZ. American artillery and air strikes "failed to check the North Vietnamese infantrymen surging down the mountain slopes," due to the large amount of foliage. As Moore ordered more of the battalion to land, the NVA automatic weapons fire increased, and a number of "troopers were killed or wounded before their helicopters touched down." Moore quickly waved off further helicopter reinforcements. The forward U.S. companies, un-

5. HORATIO A. HAWKS
Long Range Patrol 1970, Watercolor on paper, 22″ × 30″ (U.S. Army Center of Military Hist.)

6. HENRY C. CASSELLI, JR.   **In the Thick of It**   1968, Watercolor,
12″ × 19″ (U.S. Marine Corps Art Coll.)

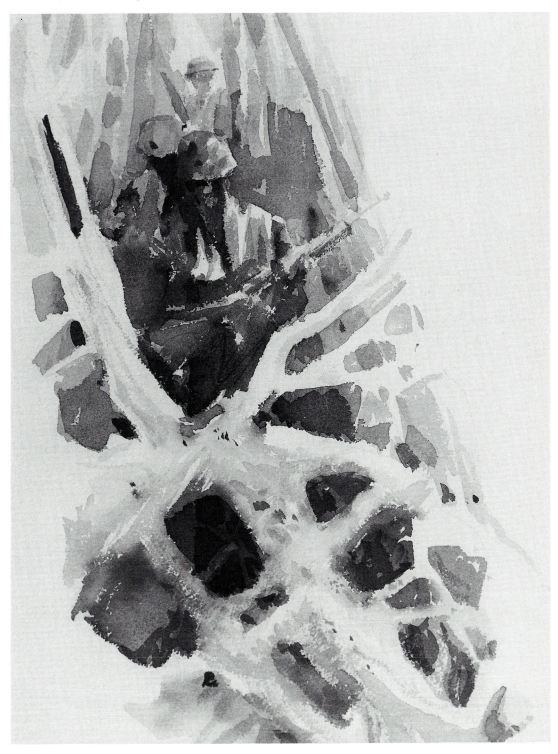

der severe fire, broke off and prepared defensive positions. One platoon of Company B found itself surrounded.[7]

Colonel Moore, aware that he was badly outnumbered, requested reinforcements and set up a defensive perimeter around X-Ray. Moore was able to land the 2nd Battalion, 7th Cavalry, and by 7:00 P.M. his command awaited an attack.

At dawn on November 15, the NVA struck Company C, and the battle at points came down to "fierce hand-to-hand fighting." By 7:45 A.M., the entire battalion was heavily engaged, and ten minutes later Moore was again requesting reinforcements. For two hours Moore's riflemen kept up their fire and held on. By 10:00 A.M. the NVA broke contact, and shortly afterwards additional U.S. troops joined the perimeter defense. Colonel Moore now launched an attack to rescue the stranded platoon. The official history of the battle graphically depicts what these cavalrymen endured.

After being cut off, Lt. Henry T. Herrick formed his men into a defensive perimeter.

7. SAMUEL E. ALEXANDER
Jungle Trail Sketch 1967, Oil crayon on paper, 14″ × 11″ (U.S. Army Center of Military Hist.)

8. THEODORE J. ABRAHAM
Jungle Waterhole 1967, Acrylic on
masonite, 23⅞″ × 19¼″ (U.S. Army
Center of Military Hist.)

9. HENRY C. CASSELLI, JR.
Stream Crossing 1967, Watercolor,
10″ × 21″ (U.S. Marine Corps Art
Coll.)

The North Vietnamese laced the small perimeter with fire so low to the ground that few of Herrick's men were able to employ their entrenching tools to provide cover. Through it all the men returned the fire, taking a heavy toll of the enemy. [Staff] Sergeant [Clyde E.] Savage [3rd squad leader,] firing his M16, hit twelve of the enemy himself during the course of the afternoon. In mid-afternoon Lieutenant Herrick was hit by a bullet which entered his hip, coursed through his body, and went out through his right shoulder. As he lay dying, the lieutenant continued to direct his perimeter defense, and in his last few moments he gave his signal operation instructions book to Staff Sergeant Carl L. Palmer, his platoon sergeant, with orders to burn it if capture seemed imminent. He told

10. SAMUEL E. ALEXANDER
Security for Engineer Operation 1967, Oil crayon on paper, 14″ × 11″ (U.S. Army Center of Military Hist.)

Palmer to redistribute the ammunition, call in artillery fire, and at the first opportunity try to make a break for it. Sergeant Palmer, himself already slightly wounded, had no sooner taken command than he too was killed.

Another squad leader took charge. He rose on his hands and knees and mumbled to no one in particular that he was going to get the platoon out of danger. He had just finished the sentence when a bullet smashed into his head. Killed in the same hail of bullets was the forward observer for the 81-mm mortar. The artillery reconnaissance sergeant, who had been traveling with the platoon, was shot in the neck. Seriously wounded, he became delirious and the men had difficulty keeping him quiet.

Sergeant Savage now took command. Snatching the artilleryman's radio, he began calling in and adjusting artillery fire. Within minutes he had ringed the perimeter with well-placed concentrations, some as close to the position as twenty meters. The fire [helped stop the overrunning of the] perimeter, but the platoon's position was still precarious. Of the 27 men in the platoon, 8 had been killed and 12 wounded, leaving less than a squad of effectives.[8]

When the relief column finally broke through the next day, they found that in addition to the "individual bravery" of the

11. JOHN O. WEHRLE **Landing Zone** 1966, Oil on canvas, 32" × 46" (U.S. Army Center of Military Hist.)

cavalrymen, Sergeant Savage's "expert use of artillery fire" had saved the cut-off platoon, for there was "not a single additional casualty after Savage had taken command."[9]

The battle for LZ X-Ray ended shortly after the relief of the cut-off platoon, as did the long campaign in the Ia Drang Valley, which officially ceased on November 26. From November 14 to November 16, Colonel Moore's force lost 79 Americans killed and 121 wounded, while the NVA left 634 bodies on the field. Casualties were high on both sides in the entire campaign. The 1st Cavalry Division lost a total of 25 percent of its authorized strength from battle and disease.

Some military writers have pointed out that the Ia Drang Valley campaign proved the feasibility of airmobility and that, despite the losses suffered by the 1st Cavalry Division, the campaign was a success. Col. Harry G. Summers, Jr., has also acknowledged the success of the army's first major battle in the Vietnam War. Summers, however, feels that this battle was crucial in contributing to the mistaken feeling on the part of Americans that "no matter what we did, we couldn't lose."[10]

Perhaps the final comment on the battle for LZ X-Ray should come from someone who fought there. Sgt. Steven

12. JAMES A. FAIRFAX
Pointman 1970, Acrylic, 34″ × 23″ (U.S. Marine Corps Art Coll.)

20

Hansen returned with an artillery unit the following year to X-Ray and found remnants of the battle, including human bones, scattered about the field. When a captain asked Sergeant Hansen how he felt about returning to the site, Hansen replied: "It gives me a funny feeling to walk around the place where so many died. In a way I'm glad we came back, but I'd still just as soon forget the whole thing."[11]

NOTES

1. Tim O'Brien, *Going After Cacciato* (New York: Delacorte Press, 1978), 301.

2. Bernard Edelman, ed., *Dear America: Letters Home from Vietnam* (New York: Bantam Books, 1985), 50.

3. Shelby L. Stanton, *Anatomy of a Division: The 1st Cav in Vietnam* (Novato, Calif.: Presidio, 1987), 47–48.

4. Ibid., 52.

5. Ibid., 55.

6. Harry G. Summers, Jr., "The Bitter Triumph of Ia Drang," *American Heritage* 35, no. 2 (February/March 1984): 53.

7. Stanton, *Anatomy of a Division*, 56.

8. John A. Cash, John Albright, and Allen W. Sandstrum, *Seven Firefights in Vietnam* (Washington, D.C.: Office of the Chief of Military History, U.S. Army, 1970), 22.

9. Ibid., 36.

10. Summers, "Ia Drang," 58.

11. Stanton, *Anatomy of a Division*, 67.

Chapter 2

LIFE IN THE REAR

Not everyone assigned to Vietnam served in combat. Every army needs supplies and support, which are as important to the outcome of a battle as infantrymen. Statistics, in fact, show that in Vietnam there were seven people in the rear echelon for every combat soldier. Almost every type of activity found in any civilian city can be found in the noncombat areas of a war, from maintaining a police force to building roads and

13. JOHN CHARLES ROACH
Short Snort, the Rock Crusher 1968, Acrylic on paper, 22″ × 20″ (U.S. Navy Combat Art Coll.)

providing a water system. Some of the combat artists devoted their works to the myriad activities of those who served away from the bush.

The accounts of most veterans of combat during the wars of the twentieth century have brought out the feeling of hostility between the combat soldier and those who serve in the rear. Soldiers' earthy language usually gives an indication of just how they view those who serve in support positions. In Vietnam, the use of an acronym says it all: to the grunts, anyone in the rear was known as a REMF (rear echelon motherfucker). The combat soldier, however, also spent time in the rear for refitting and, most important, "R and R"—rest and relaxation—and to sample some of the delights offered to soldiers serving in Southeast Asia. Both combat soldier and rear echelon soldier shared one common dream: the day when they could board the jet to take them home—the "Freedom Bird."

14. JOHN CHARLES ROACH
City Water Works, Camp Haskins, DaNang, Vietnam 1969, Acrylic on paper, 22″ × 30″ (U.S. Navy Combat Art Coll.)

Three MP's from Company "B"
   Were doing their job quite well.
They laughed at mortars, sneered at grenades;
   They were giving Charlie Hell!

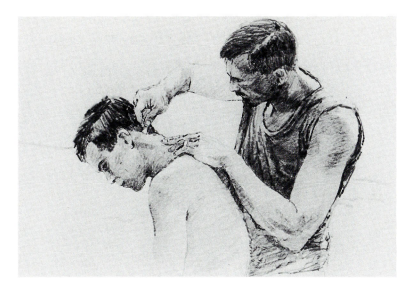

15. HENRY C.
CASSELLI, JR.
The Barber   1968, Pencil,
32″ × 44″ (U.S. Marine Corps
Art Coll.)

On static post, they were spit and polish;
    On patrol they were gung ho.
Until the night they met the beast—
    The beast that laid them low.

16. AUGUSTINE ACUNA
Donut Dollys   1966, Ink on paper,
10 ½″ × 8″ (U.S. Army Center of Military
Hist.)

25

17. EDWARD BOWEN **Camp in American Division** 1969, Oil crayon, 40″ × 60″ (U.S. Army Center of Military Hist.)

What was this horrible, awful thing
The three MP's did meet?
This awful beast that beat them down
And knocked them off their feet?

18. ROBERT K. HALLADAY **Vietnam Returnees** 1968, Acrylic, 22″ × 30″ (U.S. Marine Corps Art Coll.)

26

19. CLIFF YOUNG **Village Sick Call** 1969, Acrylic, 20″ × 29½″
(U.S. Navy Combat Art Coll.)

LIFE IN THE REAR

An enemy weapon, a VC trap?
    Did Charlie hit from the rear?
It was none of these things, my son, my son:
    It was only Vietnamese beer.
                    —John Horn, "The Ballad of the Beast," in
            Forest L. Kimler, ed., *Boondock Bards* (San Francisco:
                                Stars and Stripes, 1968), 37

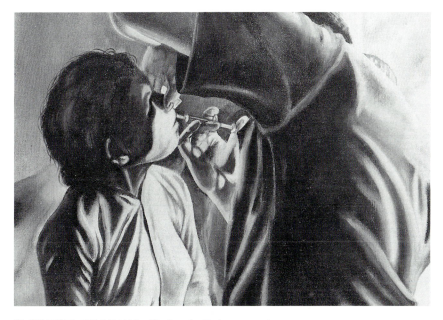

20. WALTER GIORDANO **Easing the Pain** 1969, Oil on canvas, 16″ × 20″ (U.S.
Navy Combat Art Coll.)

FORGOTTEN WARRIORS

21. STEPHEN H. SHELDON
Morale Booster 1967, Oil on canvas,
30″ × 22″ (U.S. Army Center of Military
Hist.)

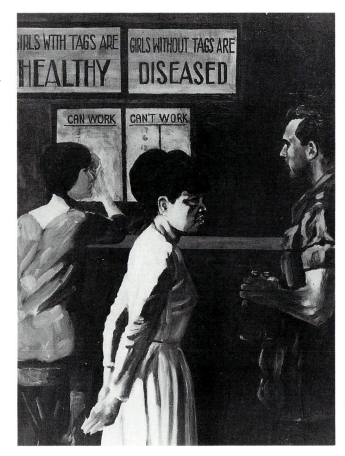

22. HOUSTON STIFF
Dear Mom 1968, Colored inks (U.S.
Marine Corps Art Coll.)

28

23. JAMES R. BUTCHER **It's Over** 1968, Mixed media (U.S. Marine Corps Art Coll.)

Chapter 3

ENDURANCE

Soldiers in the bush fought two wars. One was against a human enemy that could bring sudden death or painful injuries. This war usually came in short but very intense periods. The terrain and environment, however, caused the longest sustained war for the grunts. While a helicopter could quickly lift an infantryman to a landing zone, once on the ground the soldier soon

24. PETER COPELAND
Search and Destroy Mission 1967,
Watercolor on paper, 11″ × 14″ (U.S.
Army Center of Military Hist.)

had to fight the strength-sapping heat and humidity. Depending on where he was operating, the grunt could face climbing steep mountains, walking miles through dense jungles, and wading through swampy terrain, all in temperatures that could reach one hundred degrees and while carrying loads of seventy pounds or more. The war with terrain and environment was constant, with very little relief. Some of the combat artists who accompanied the troops into the bush masterfully caught this war of endurance and its effects on the young men who were forced to live through it. Augustine Acuna's *Dog Tired* (Illus. 29) makes one feel the utter exhaustion of soldiers on patrol. Victory Von Reynolds' *Riding Back from Patrol* (Illus. 33) graphically depicts what the combination of anxiety, heat, humidity, and terrain could do to a soldier. In Richard L. Yaco's *Bombcrater* (Illus. 36) the heat is almost palpable. Writers such as Tim O'Brien and Michael Herr also have been able to capture the effects of the war of

25. HENRY C. CASSELLI, JR.
Loaded Down 1968, Pencil,
24″ × 28″ (U.S. Marine Corps Art
Coll.)

endurance on soldiers. This chapter will allow the reader to grasp just how much a grunt had to endure in the bush.

The soldier in the field carried heavy loads up steep mountains and through heat, the water of the Delta region, rice paddies, elephant grass, and the driving rain of the monsoons. There were no air conditioned post exchanges or clubs to relax in or even the most simple amenities. One soldier wrote that they carried "nothing but a razor and a bar of soap for comfort, wear[ing] only the clothes we have and wash[ing] them in

26. HENRY C. CASSELLI, JR. **Radio-op** 1968, Pencil, 22″ × 28″ (U.S. Marine Corps Art Coll.)

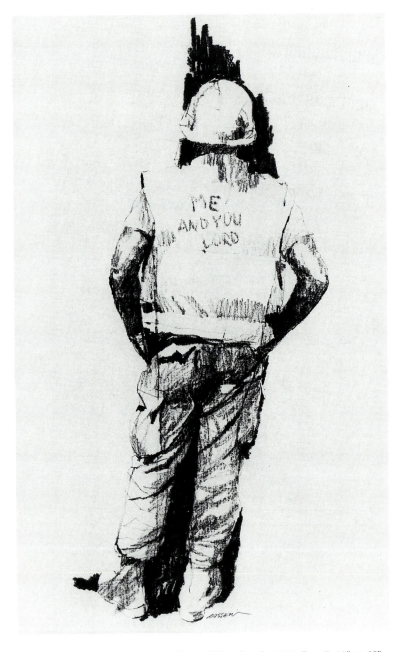

27. HENRY C. CASSELLI, JR.   **Me and You Lord**   1969, Pencil, 19″ × 25″
(U.S. Marine Corps Art Coll.)

28. WALTER GIORDANO **Hell** 1969, Oil on canvas, 36″ × 18″
(U.S. Navy Combat Art Coll.)

rivers and streams as we cross them."[1] Another wrote that anyone patrolling in elephant grass ought to receive the Purple Heart for wounds because the foliage possessed razor-sharp edges. Probably the best description of life in the bush during the monsoon season comes from a letter written by a young army ranger after returning from a three-day patrol. "Someday climb into the shower with all your clothes on, stay there three days under the water, shutting it off every now and then, and you'll have a reasonably good idea of what it's like in the boonies during the seasonal rains. I looked like a prune by the time we came back."[2]

The fauna of South Vietnam did not make life any easier for those in the field. Men new to Vietnam were told of the deadly "two step" snakes—if bitten you had two steps before you fell dead—along with stories of cobras and tigers. The insect life also left something to be desired. One marine wrote that he had "about 42 mosquito bites on my left forearm."[3] O'Brien, in *Going After Cacciato*, graphically allows the reader to glimpse what one soldier endured in Vietnam.

29. AUGUSTINE ACUNA
Dog Tired 1966, Pencil on board, 18″ × 22″ (U.S. Army Center of Military Hist.)

30. AUGUSTINE ACUNA **The Grind** 1966, Pencil on board, 30″ × 20″ (U.S. Army Center of Military Hist.)

31. LEONARD H. DERMOTT **Hot Feet** 1966, Watercolor, 18″ × 24″ (U.S. Marine Corps Art Coll.)

The rain grew fungus that grew in the men's boots and socks, and their socks rotted, and their feet turned white and soft so that the skin could be scraped off with fingernails, and Harris woke up screaming one night with a leech on his tongue. When it was not raining, a low mist moved, . . . blending the elements into a single grey element, and the war was cold and pasty and rotten. . . . The ammunition corroded and the foxholes filled with mud water during the nights. . . . [4]

The terrain, the weather, the long days carrying—"humping," in the jargon—packs and weapons, all led to a state of exhaustion that is difficult for most Americans to imagine. Both combat artists and perceptive writers have attempted to capture one of the largest aspects of a combat soldier's life: the complete and utter tiredness of fighting the environment. Michael Herr describes the exhaustion in *Dispatches*:

Every day people were dying there because of some small detail they could not be bothered to observe. Imagine being too tired to snap a flak jacket closed, too tired to clean your rifle, too tired to guard a light, too tired to deal with a half-inch margin of safety that moving through the war often demanded, just too fucking tired and then dying behind that exhaustion. [5]

32. CHARLES
WATERHOUSE
Night Watch [n.d.] Acrylic
on board, 18″ × 24½″ (U.S.
Navy Combat Art Coll.)

38

33. VICTORY VON REYNOLDS   **Riding Back from Patrol**   1969, Oil,
48″ × 54″ (U.S. Army Center of Military Hist.)

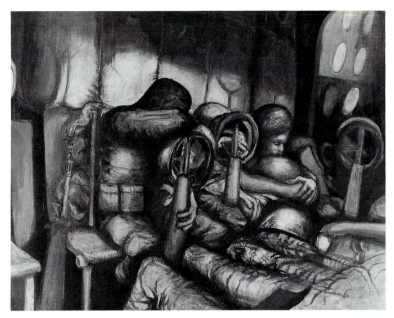

34. EDWARD BOWEN
Soldier on C–130 1969, Oil
on canvas, 48″ × 54″ (U.S.
Army Center of Military Hist.)

35. HOUSTON STIFF   **Artilleryman**   1968, Acrylic, 16″ × 24″ (U.S. Marine Corps Art Coll.)

36. RICHARD L. YACO **Bombcrater** 1968, Acrylic, 24″ × 32⅞″ (U.S. Marine Corps Art Coll.)

37. HOUSTON STIFF **90% Boredom** 1967, Felt-tip pen, (U.S. Marine Corps Art Coll.)

41

NOTES

1. Bernard Edelman, ed., *Dear America: Letters Home from Vietnam* (New York: Bantam Books, 1985), 40.

2. Ibid., 64.

3. Ibid., 46.

4. Tim O'Brien, *Going After Cacciato* (New York: Delacorte Press, 1978), 13.

5. Michael Herr, *Dispatches* (New York: Alfred A. Knopf, 1977), 54.

Chapter 4

THE SOLDIERS

The combat artists of the Vietnam War excelled in depicting three aspects of the war: the soldiers themselves; combat situations; and the compassion and camaraderie of those who fought. This chapter concerns the first of these three areas: the portrayal of the men who fought the war. The subjects of the first works shown are the special or elite troops used in Vietnam, for example, the U.S. Navy's SEALs (Sea, Air, Land). Some almost suggest the kind of illustrations used in recruiting new troops. One can, for example, imagine James Butcher's *RECON Dude* (Illus. 39) and Howard Terpning's *The Leader* (Illus. 40) gracing U.S. Marine Corps recruiting posters. James G. Scott's and Trella Koczwara's works capture the

38. JAMES R. DRAKE
On a Long Range Patrol 1969, Watercolor on paper, 20″ × 28½″ (U.S. Army Center of Military Hist.)

RECON 'DUDE' DASHES
FROM CHOPPER
9 JAN 68

39. JAMES R. BUTCHER **RECON Dude** 1968, Pencil (U.S. Marine Corps Art Coll.)

40. HOWARD TERPNING **The Leader** 1968, Acrylic, 18″ × 24″ (U.S. Marine Corps Art Coll.)

sense of stealth that seems to emanate from these special operations troops. It is sensitivity to the average combat soldier, however, that makes the combat artist excel. For instance, look closely at the works of Henry C. Casselli, Jr., in this chapter to see how war changes the faces of youth. Read the closing passage by Michael Herr, and then once again look at the faces of the soldiers depicted herein.

The Vietnam War added new names to the lexicon of war. Elite troops, such as Green Berets, SEALs, RECON Marines, and others, caught the imagination of the media and the general public. The men who served with these units fought and endured as much as any soldier and, because most were professional soldiers, they spent many tours in Southeast Asia. One former Special Forces soldier turned novelist described a Green Beret veteran:

41. CHARLES
WATERHOUSE
**U.S. Navy SEAL, Aboard
Green Cow** [n.d.], Oil on
board, 9½″ × 13½″ (U.S.
Navy Combat Art Coll.)

[Sergeant Major] had a slight Southern accent that was very pleasant. . . . And no one had ever heard Sergeant Major raise his voice above the level of polite conversation, even in a firefight. In combat he used hand signals to direct his Chinese Nung bodyguards.

There was a knotted rope of scar around Sergeant Major's ankles, as if he had worn leg irons for years on a chain gang. All the old Southeast Asia hands had the ankle scars. They are from the leeches.[1]

It is easy to understand why the exploits of these highly trained men captured the interest of the public. For example, Mike Beamon, a former SEAL, gave this recollection of his team's efforts to escape detection from a pursuing patrol: "Our only hope was to make ourselves look like a pile of logs. So we became a pile of logs. It's incredible to explain what you can become, the illusion that you can present to people. You can become a bush, a log, if you just concentrate hard enough on being that."[2]

Americans, brought up on war movies, perceived combat as a face-to-face encounter. The small screen, however, showed men firing round after round of automatic rifle fire,

42. JAMES G. SCOTT
Chief Rusi 1969,
Watercolor, 18¼″ × 24¾″
(U.S. Navy Combat Art Coll.)

accompanied by the sounds of low-flying jets dropping bombs, but very few sightings of an enemy in combat. The published exploits of the unconventional forces were exciting to read and seemed almost like a John Wayne movie come to life. In short, this was something much easier for the public to grasp than the reality of the actual war. The perceptions of the general public of what these unconventional warriors accomplished, of course, do not always reflect reality.

It was, however, the average combat soldier who received the most sympathy from various artists in Vietnam, simply because of the grunt's youth. John Groth, a combat artist who covered at least four wars, once remarked, "In every war you see the same guys fighting—the eighteen- and nineteen-year-olds—all with the same look."[3] It is capturing this look, one of complete exhaustion, and something else, coming from the young-old face of an eighteen-year-old, that combat artists do best. Examine, for example, Henry C. Casselli, Jr.'s portraits

43. TRELLA KOCZWARA **1st RECON** 1970, Oil, 67″ × 82″ (U.S. Marine Corp Art Coll.)

44. JAMES S. HARDY **Old Guard** 1969, Ink on paper, 10½″ × 14½″ (U.S. Army Center of Military Hist.)

45. PETER COPELAND
Member of 101st Airborne 1967, Watercolor on paper, 14″ × 11″ (U.S. Army Center of Military Hist.)

to understand the youth of the men who fought the war, and then compare them to Casselli's works on the marines in Hue, in chapter 5, to see the effects of combat on young men.

I saw that face at least a thousand times at a hundred bases and camps, all the youth sucked out of the eyes, the color drawn from the skin, cold white lips, you knew he wouldn't wait for any of it to come back. Life had made him old, he'd live it out old. . . . (How do you feel when a nineteen-year-old kid tells you from the bottom of his heart that he's gotten too old for this kind of shit?)[4]

46. HENRY C. CASSELLI, JR. **Portrait Sketch** 1968, Pencil, 12″ × 25″ (U.S. Marine Corps Art Coll.)

NOTES

1. Kent Anderson, *Sympathy for the Devil* (Garden City, N.Y.: Doubleday, 1987), 37–38. "The Nungs are a tribal group originally from the area near the North Vietnamese–Chinese border" that fielded an entire division during the French and early Diem years. "They were not active again until the CIA and the Special Forces recruited them to serve as personal bodyguards for the SF [Special Forces] teams in the new CIDG [Civilian Irregular Defense Group] teams." Charles M. Simpson III, *Inside the Green Berets: The First Thirty Years. A History of the U.S. Army Special Forces* (Novato, Calif.: Presidio Press, 1983), 124.

2. Al Santoli, *Everything We Had: An Oral History of the Vietnam War by Thirty-Three Soldiers Who Fought It* (New York: Random House, 1981), 210.

3. Quoted in Joseph F. Anzenberger, ed., *Combat Art of the Vietnam War* (Jefferson, N.C.: McFarland and Co., 1986), 12.

4. Michael Herr, *Dispatches* (New York: Alfred A. Knopf, 1977), 16.

47. HENRY C. CASSELLI, JR. **Thinking** 1967, Pencil, 18″ × 24″ (U.S. Marine Corps Art Coll.)

48. GARY W. MOSS **Marine in Thought** 1970, Watercolor, 20″ × 25″ (U.S. Marine Corps Art Coll.)

Chapter 5

CONTACT: THE EFFECTS
OF COMBAT

This chapter deals with the second area in which the combat artists excel: depicting the actual periods of combat—contact in the jargon—or combat situations. In most cases, the artists did not show the actual fighting. After all, it is extremely difficult to be sketching while bullets are flying about or high explosives are landing nearby, although some artists did exactly this. What many of the artists recorded was the start of combat; the results are left to the imagination of the viewer. This is one of the most effective ways to depict the war. Benjamin Long's *Snipers in Hedgerow* (Illus. 77) gives one the feeling of a small unit about to attack; one can almost see the marines charging across the open spaces to the hedgerow. Howard Terpning's *Moving Up* (Illus. 78) makes us see "the enemy" we are about to face, even though he is not shown in the picture. John T. Dyer, Jr.'s *Sky of Khe Sanh* (Illus. 64) brings out the sense of impending disaster that seemed to prevail over the siege of Khe Sanh. Houston Stiff's *Khe Sanh Crouch* (Illus. 66) gives the reader the best feeling of the constant incoming artillery rounds that the defenders of that beleaguered base endured.

Much of the combat in Vietnam occurred at night. Old Southeast Asia hands repeated the cliché, "The night belongs to Charlie [the Viet Cong]." Charles Waterhouse and Walter Giordano, among others, catch the almost primordial fear of the night, to which is added the strange illumination of the darkness brought about by modern war. Look closely, again, at Henry C. Casselli's works showing the exhaustion of the marines in Hue to see what war entails, and then at Leonard H. Dermott's grim *Perimeter Wire* (Illus. 73) to see the final results of combat. It is the ability of the artists to have the

53

viewer "see" combat, without actually picturing it, plus the portrayal of the effects of combat upon those who must face it, that makes the works contained within this chapter exceptional. Much of the narrative of this chapter deals with combat. The reader should, however, after reading the descriptions of fighting in the old Imperial City of Hue, study Casselli's works. Or read Michael Herr's description of a night patrol and then reexamine the art dealing with night to obtain the full import of this chapter.

Combat in South Vietnam took place on all types of terrain. What many today may not realize is that some large engagements took place in urban areas. One of the most intense battles in the Vietnam War for the U.S. Marine Corps, for example, took place within a city.

On January 31, 1968, the second day of the Vietnamese holiday of Tet, at least two battalions of the 6th North Vietnamese (NVA) Regiment struck the city of Hue and gained control of the old Imperial City, except for two pockets of

49. HOWARD TERPNING
Touchdown 1968, Acrylic,
22" × 30" (U.S. Marine
Corps Art Coll.)

50. LEONARD H. DERMOTT **Line of Departure** 1967, Acrylic (U.S. Marine Corps Art Coll.)

resistance, one held by South Vietnamese troops and the other by U.S. troops in the U.S. Military Advisory Compound. At first, the marine command at Phu Bai, eight miles to the south, thought that the attacking force was small, so it sent only a single company in response. Company A, 1st Battalion, 1st Marines ran headlong into one of the NVA battalions, and soon messages for reinforcement were being sent. Over the next three weeks, three more companies, three command groups, and a tank platoon—a total of about 1,000 marines—were needed to dislodge the NVA and VC.[1] The battle eventually became "the longest and bloodiest ground action of the Tet Offensive and . . . [the] bloodiest single action" of the war to that date.[2]

Marines and South Vietnamese troops faced vicious house to house fighting in a gloomy, cold drizzle while being subjected to almost constant sniper fire. Most of the Leathernecks were accustomed to fighting only in the countryside and had to learn the hard lessons of street fighting. Veteran marines compared the fighting with the Korean War: "Seoul was tough, but this . . . it's something else." By the end of the first week of intense combat the Americans had retaken less than half of the city while receiving at least 250 casualties.[3]

51. MICHAEL R. CROOK
Search and Destroy 1967,
Watercolor on paper,
14″ × 20″ (U.S. Army Center of Military Hist.)

The marines advanced slowly through the city, while confused, homeless civilians wandered the streets. The dead lay everywhere. A correspondent wrote: "A woman knelt in death by a wall in the corner of her garden. A child lay on stairs crushed by a fallen roof. Many of the bodies had turned black and begun to decompose, and rats gnawed at the exposed flesh." The fighting cost the attackers greatly. One estimate stated that the "Marines took one casualty for every meter of ground gained."[4] One of the most wrenching photographs to come out of this battle is that of a tank carrying dead and wounded marines out of Hue. In a rarity for the Vietnam War, some marines began to show a form of shell shock under the intense pressure of this fight.

Army units from the 1st Air Cavalry Division and the 101st Airborne Division were fed into the battle. They also paid a high price: the units lost as many men in five days as the marines had lost in the past three weeks. The battle for Hue ended on February 25, 1968. The enemy had lost an estimated 5,000 killed and 89 captured. Americans had lost 216 killed

52. MICHAEL P. PALA
Patrol   1968, Watercolor and pencil, 17¾″ × 12″
(U.S. Army Center of Military Hist.)

and 1,364 seriously wounded, and South Vietnamese forces lost 384 killed and 1,830 wounded. Approximately 5,800 civilians had been killed in the battle or executed by the NVA or VC.[5]

Another aspect of the war that may be unfamiliar to contemporary Americans deals with sieges at dug-in positions. The most written-about engagement remains Khe Sanh, which television commentators and journalists of the day compared to the French attempt to defend Dien Bien Phu. In fact, the specter of the French defeat permeated news reports and haunted the minds of some military men as well as President Lyndon Johnson, who had a model of Khe Sanh erected in the situation room in the basement of the White House to refer to as he read the daily reports from the base.

Some 6,000 marines faced an estimated 20,000–40,000 NVA regulars for seventy-seven days. General Westmoreland ordered massive air strikes to break the back of the attackers. In Operation Niagara, Westmoreland had more than 2,000 strike aircraft and over 300 sorties flown per day. Huge B–52 bombers flew 2,548 sorties and dropped 59,542 tons of bombs. Added to this incredible bombardment was artillery support.[6]

Despite the massive use of bombs, artillery shells, and supplies, the 6,000 marines, and some Special Forces troops located nearby, still faced the very real possibility of fighting the NVA in a massive assault. In fact, it was the Special Forces camp that received the awaited massed attack. The NVA used

53. DENNIS O. McGEE
Mine Clearing
Operation 1967, Ink on
paper, 12″ × 17¾″ (U.S.
Army Center of Military Hist.)

54. AUGUSTINE ACUNA **Roundup and Questioning of Villagers—1966** 1966, Watercolor, 18″ × 28″ (U.S. Army Center of Military Hist.)

55. ALEXANDER A. BOGDANOVICH **Airborne Above Dead VC** 1966, Acrylic on board, 29¾″ × 33″ (U.S. Army Center of Military Hist.)

59

a weapon that many Americans do not realize was deployed against U.S. troops: Soviet tanks.

Lang Vie, located some seven miles southwest of Khe Sanh, was a strongly defended camp, ringed by a three-layer barbed-wire barrier some fifty meters wide, with claymore mines. Bunkers within the camp were heavily sandbagged on all sides.

The camp's firepower was impressive. Two 4.2-inch mortars, with over 800 high-explosive and illumination rounds,

56. WENDELL A. PARKS **The Sniper** 1968, Pen and ink, 14″ × 16″ (U.S. Marine Corps Art Coll.)

provided heavy indirect fire support for the camp. Each company and platoon area had one 81-mm mortar for which 2,000 assorted rounds of ammunition were available. Nineteen 60-mm mortars were positioned strategically throughout the camp, with nearly 3,000 high-explosive rounds. There had been ominous rumors and reports of NVA tanks in the area. Even this unexpected development could be met, for the camp had two 106-mm recoilless rifles, with each weapon having more than twenty high-explosive rounds. As a supplement, there were four 57-mm recoilless rifles, with over 3,000 rounds. For close-in tank defense, there were one hundred light assault weapons (LAWs), one-shot, disposable launcher-containers loaded with a shaped charged round and fired from the shoulder.

The camp commander, Capt. Frank C. Willoughby, could call upon 105-mm, 155-mm, and 175-mm artillery support from the marine base at Khe Sanh and other locations. In addition, he could call upon air support and request two rifle companies from the 26th Marine Regiment at Khe Sanh. For manpower, Captain Willoughby had 24 Americans, mostly

57. HENRY C. CASSELLI, JR. **Two on Point** 1968, Pencil, 22″ × 28″ (U.S. Marine Corps Art Coll.)

U.S. Army Special Forces, and 500 indigenous troops, known as the Civilian Irregular Defense Group (CIDG).[7]

Approximately thirty minutes after midnight on February 7, NVA forces struck Lang Vie. Sgt. Nikolas Fragas, manning an observation post, radioed Captain Willoughby: "We have two tanks in our wire!"[8]

Col. Daniel F. Schungel, visiting the camp from Da Nang, told Willoughby to concentrate as much artillery and air support as possible and to request help from the marines at Khe Sanh. Colonel Schungel then went out of the bunker to help organize teams to knock out the Soviet PT76 tanks.

The tanks began to lumber through the wire, supported by artillery and approximately 400 NVA infantry. The foot soldiers found their targets with the help of searchlights mounted on the tanks. The camp fought back. Sfc. James W. Holt trained a 106-mm recoilless rifle on the lead tanks and scored direct hits on two machines. A third tank appeared around the two blazing tanks.

By a little over one hour into the battle, the NVA controlled the eastern portion of the camp, and the situation was critical. Even though the Special Forces and CIDG troops had managed to knock out the first three tanks, others came clanking

58. HENRY C. CASSELLI, JR. **Marines in Hue** 1968, Pencil, 22″ × 18″ (U.S. Marine Corps Art Coll.)

62

59. HENRY C. CASSELLI, JR.   **Exhausted**   1968, Pencil, 22″ × 28″ (U.S. Marine Corps Art Coll.)

60. HENRY C. CASSELLI, JR.   **Chi-Town**   1968, Pencil, 22″ × 28″ (U.S. Marine Corps Art Coll.)

61. HENRY C. CASSELLI, JR.   **Marine in the City of Hue**   1968, Pencil (U.S. Marine Corps Art Coll.)

from the north and west, with a total of eleven committed to the fight. Some of the NVA following the tanks were armed with flamethrowers. Two of the tanks moved to within ten meters of the command bunker and began to fire, then one rolled onto the roof. NVA sappers then threw satchel charges and grenades into the bunker's vents. Captain Willoughby had all lights turned off in the bunker and called in artillery fire close to his position. He asked the marines to send reinforcements to relieve the camp. Col. David E. Lownds, the marine commander of Khe Sanh, however, did not dare make a night helicopter assault against tanks, and he felt that his Leathernecks would be ambushed if sent overland, so he refused the request. Lang Vie would have to hold out until daylight.

The fighting continued, and in the cold light of the flares a confused scene was played out with tanks, NVA infantry, U.S. Special Forces, and CIDG troops moving among the heavy fire. The nature of the battle can be glimpsed from an edited transcript of the radio traffic from Lang Vie made by 1LT Paul R. Longgrear, a participant in the engagement:

62. JOHN T. DYER, JR.
Special Forces Camp, Khe Sanh 1968, Pen and ink
(U.S. Marine Corps Art Coll.)

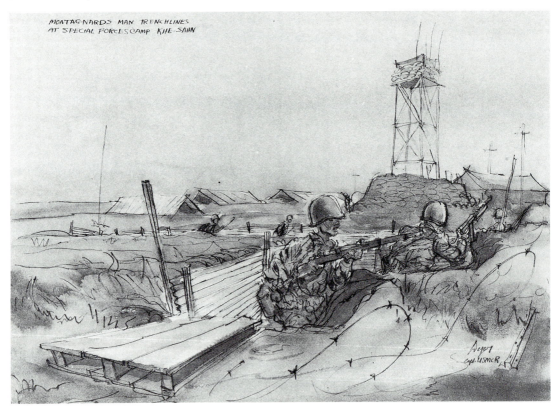

MONTAGNARDS MAN TRENCHLINES AT SPECIAL FORCES CAMP KHE-SAHN

0128: *SP5 William G. McMurray and Ssgt. Dennis L. Thompson (28B) to 06 (Captain Willoughby):* "Troops are moving up on this position from two directions."

0132: *28B to 06:* "I think the enemy is in our old bunkers. Get some HE in there."

0136: *32B (Sgt. Richard H. Allen):* "Christ, a bomb just fell on our position!"

Sfc. Earl F. Burke (40): "There are two tanks on the road to Khe Sanh."

Unknown: "Can you get the LAW over here?"

Unknown: "We don't have anymore LAWs left."

0200: *06 to 09:* "I think we got a tank down by the dispensary. There is another by supply. We didn't get it. There's one by supply."

CONTACT

63. JOHN T. DYER, JR.
Trenchline—Khe Sanh
1968, Felt-tip pen (U.S. Marine Corps Art Coll.)

67

0209: *09 to FAC (Forward Air Controller, in aircraft)*: "We have a very active tank on each end of the camp."

0210: *09 to FAC*: "Tanks and a lot of infantry are coming into the camp!"

0215: *09 to FAC*: "They are coming in from each end of the camp. We will have to do something soon!"

0221: *09 to 06*: "Those tanks are tearing up 104 Company!"

0223: *09 to 06*: "Tanks coming our way!"

0227: *09 to FAC*: "There is a tank coming up on the TOC (tactical operations center)!"

0230: *09 to 06*: There is a tank right on top of the TOC and it's giving us fits! We knocked one out."

0245: *FAC to 09*: "Where do you want the bombs?"

09 to FAC: "Put the bombs just south of the green star cluster to get the tank. We're moving off the hill." [Last transmission from Lang Vie.][9]

Lang Vie could not hold out against the combination of tanks and determined NVA infantry. Of the 500 CIDG troops, 200 were dead or missing, with 75 wounded. Ten of the 24 Americans at the camp were killed.[10]

64. JOHN T. DYER, JR. **Sky of Khe Sanh** 1968, Mixed media, 17″ × 24″ (U.S. Marine Corps Art Coll.)

Michael Herr captured what must have been on the minds of many of the defenders at Khe Sanh when he asked, after Lang Vie, How could a marine look out of his "perimeter at night without hearing the treads coming?"[11] The attack on the Special Forces camp seemed to demonstrate that if the enemy wanted to take Khe Sanh they would come in waves until the base was overrun.

Yet the awaited mass attack never came. Instead the marines of Khe Sanh had enemy artillery trained on them, with between 50 and 500 rounds of incoming per day, causing one defender to compare the experience of never knowing when a round would land to "sitting in an electric chair and waiting for someone to pull the switch."[12] One visitor to the base recalled the toll this constant bombardment took on the marines: "It was never easy to guess the ages of the Marines at Khe Sanh since nothing like youth ever lasted in their faces for very long. It was the eyes. Because they were always either strained or blazed-out or simply blank, they never had anything to do with what the rest of the face was doing."[13]

The incoming artillery led to what was known as the "Khe Sanh crouch" or "shuffle." One former Khe Sanh veteran related what the shuffle consisted of when he was trying to get aboard a C–123 out of the base. "You looked the way you were going, and you never went more then fifty meters in one

65. WALTER GIORDANO
Sentinel DMZ 1969, Oil on canvas, 24″ × 30″ (U.S. Navy Combat Art Coll.)

shot," recalled Lcpl. Phil Mineer. "It was a half-slouch combined with the opposite of being cross-eyed: "One eye always looked where you were going and the other always looked at an alternate route, where you would go if the rounds came in."[14]

To supply the cut-off base, transport planes made more than 450 flights into Khe Sanh; when weather was poor, helicopters felt their way into the landing strip to bring in replacements and supplies and to carry out the wounded and the dead. The pilots of both transports and helicopters faced a deadly gauntlet of small arms and anti-aircraft fire; in addition, these aircraft were very large targets for the artillery pieces while on the ground. Pilots performed incredible feats of airmanship in landing and made record times in unloading cargo. The C–123 Provider, for example, could make a very steep approach to the airstrip. Once on the ground the craft rarely came to a complete halt. "The pilot drove his plane like a truck through the unloading area, the cargo master rolled one-ton pallets off the open tail gate, and the plane turned for takeoff."[15]

Now came the difficult time for marines and others who were due to rotate out of Khe Sanh. In the final few seconds before the C–123 took off, the men who were departing had to leap from the trenches near the airstrip and run through the inevitable shellfire toward the moving aircraft. "It was a sprint of terror, with cries and shouts and the mad jouncing of equipment and a final desperate leap for the Provider's gaping jaw. The adrenalin rush soaked some of the passengers in sweat; others lay face down on the floor, crying, 'Thank God, Jesus Christ, thank God.' "[16]

The normal time on the ground for the C–123 was an extremely short three minutes, but some pilots managed to do the turnaround in an incredible one minute. Of course, once the plane began its ascent it once again had to face flak and small arms fire.

Near the end of March a marine patrol discovered a series of NVA trenches leading toward Khe Sanh. In the siege of Dien Bien Phu, the Viet Minh had used this tactic to get as close to the French positions as possible before attacking. General Westmoreland called for B–52 strikes, which dropped their large load of bombs just outside the perimeter.

The NVA continued their digging. Some trenches were as close as one hundred yards to the marine positions and were T-shaped, which usually meant that the NVA were at the stage to attack. As March 13, the anniversary of the Battle of Dien Bien Phu, approached, the marines girded for the attack they thought was inevitable. The thirteenth came and passed and nothing happened. By the end of the month, patrols found that the trenches were abandoned and the NVA gone. The siege of Khe Sanh was officially over on April 8.

Why the North Vietnamese failed to attack Khe Sanh remains unknown. As with most aspects of the war, a number of reasons have been put forth. Two of the most common are that the abandonment of the siege was related to the failure of the NVA to hold Hue and other areas, and that Khe Sanh was never a major target, merely a feint designed to lure American troops, supplies, and attention away from the cities during the Tet offensive. Once that was accomplished, there was no need to continue the siege. In any event, the frustration of the war is reflected in the action at this lonely outpost. For over three months, the attention of almost everyone in the government, from the president downward, as well as that of the media, was riveted upon Khe Sanh. Two months after the siege was lifted, however, the bunkers were blown up, the area leveled, and the troops withdrawn.

66. HOUSTON STIFF
Khe Sanh Crouch 1968, Acrylic (U.S. Marine Corps Art Coll.)

Less well-known than Khe Sanh was an area with the lilting name of Con Thien, known to missionaries as the Hill of Angels. Located two miles from the Demilitarized Zone (DMZ), Con Thien was a bulldozed plateau 160 meters high. Ringed by barbed wire and crisscrossed with trenches and sandbag-covered bunkers, it was large enough to hold only the understrengthened 1st Battalion, 9th Marines. The importance of this small outpost was that it helped guard the McNamara Line and overlooked a principal enemy supply route into South Vietnam as well as the U.S. supply complex at Dong Ha, ten miles away.[17] (The McNamara Line was a series of strong points near the Demilitarized Zone intended to stop infiltration into South Vietnam.)

67. WENDELL A. PARKS
The Bunker [n.d.], Pencil, 15″ × 18″ (U.S. Marine Corps Art Coll.)

Enemy artillery batteries were hidden in caves in the northern hills of the DMZ. The guns, protected from air strikes by the caves, were rolled out to fire, and were frequently shifted to prevent U.S. spotters from calling down air strikes on them. In addition to "blazing heat and choking dust, . . . snipers and threats of ground attack," the marine defenders endured hundreds of rounds of incoming artillery each day. Over one six-day period, for example, the base was slammed with a total of more than 3,000 rounds of artillery, rockets, and mortars. On September 25, 1967, more than 1,200 rounds fell on the base. David Douglas Duncan's photographs of Con Thien show the bleak and barren wasteland caused by this constant shelling.[18]

The shelling took its toll, and the men began to call themselves "the walking dead." Duncan recalled:

Every Marine journeyed through each night in his own way, with stops at memories of home, plans for the future and fantasy after fantasy where every chrome-plated deal worked. He lived in the sustaining world of a combat infantryman's imagination, shielded and reassured by the silent presence of another Marine in the trench beside him, or the next foxhole, whose dreams were probably interchangeable with his own.[19]

The siege for the marines inside Con Thien was indeed difficult, but the heaviest fighting took place outside of the wire, as marines tried to prevent the NVA from completely encircling the site. As early as July 2, an NVA ambush killed 275 Americans. This set off a series of violent attacks and counterattacks, climaxing on July 6 with a strong American ground attack backed by gunships, tanks, naval gunfire, artillery, and just about every other means of delivering high explosives upon an enemy. By the end of this devastating whirlwind, there were 800 NVA dead and tons of equipment destroyed.

Yet, these losses did not seem to slow down the fierce ground attacks. General Westmoreland then sent in four marine battalions to circle Con Thien and, in Operation Neutralize, delivered "one of the greatest concentrations of firepower in the Vietnam War." The large amount of high explosives finally broke the back of the NVA ground attacks. By the end of September the shelling began to slacken, and on October 4, General Westmoreland announced that the siege of Con Thien was over.[20]

Incoming rockets and mortars could make the toughest soldier pause to reflect. But nighttime brought a new meaning to the word *fear*. In the dark tropical night the VC and NVA seemed able to come through the wire like ghosts. Kent Anderson, in *Sympathy for the Devil*, describes the abilities of Vietnamese sappers to breach defenses that seemed impregnable.

68. CHARLES WATERHOUSE **Hunter** 1969, Acrylic (U.S. Navy Combat Art Coll.)

69. LARRY ZABEL **Ambush** 1969, Oil on canvas, 18″ × 24″ (U.S. Navy Combat Art Coll.)

74

The sappers, [wearing only loincloths,] covered themselves with ash so they would not reflect light, and it gave them a ghostly appearance. . . . [As they slithered through the wire,] [f]reckles of blood began to appear through the ash as they nicked and cut themselves on the wire.

They moved very slowly, feeling ahead of them for trip flares and claymore mines. . . . When they came to pebble-filled beer cans that were hung on the wire as noise-makers, they simply dropped in a handful of dirt to muffle them. The North Vietnamese sappers were brave soldiers who were very good at a dangerous job. An elbow or ankle could trip a flare, ruin the attack, and ensure their deaths in the bubbling smoking silver light of the magnesium flares.[21]

70. LEONARD H. DERMOTT
Inside the DMZ 1967, Casein, 18″ × 24″ (U.S. Marine Corps Art Coll.)

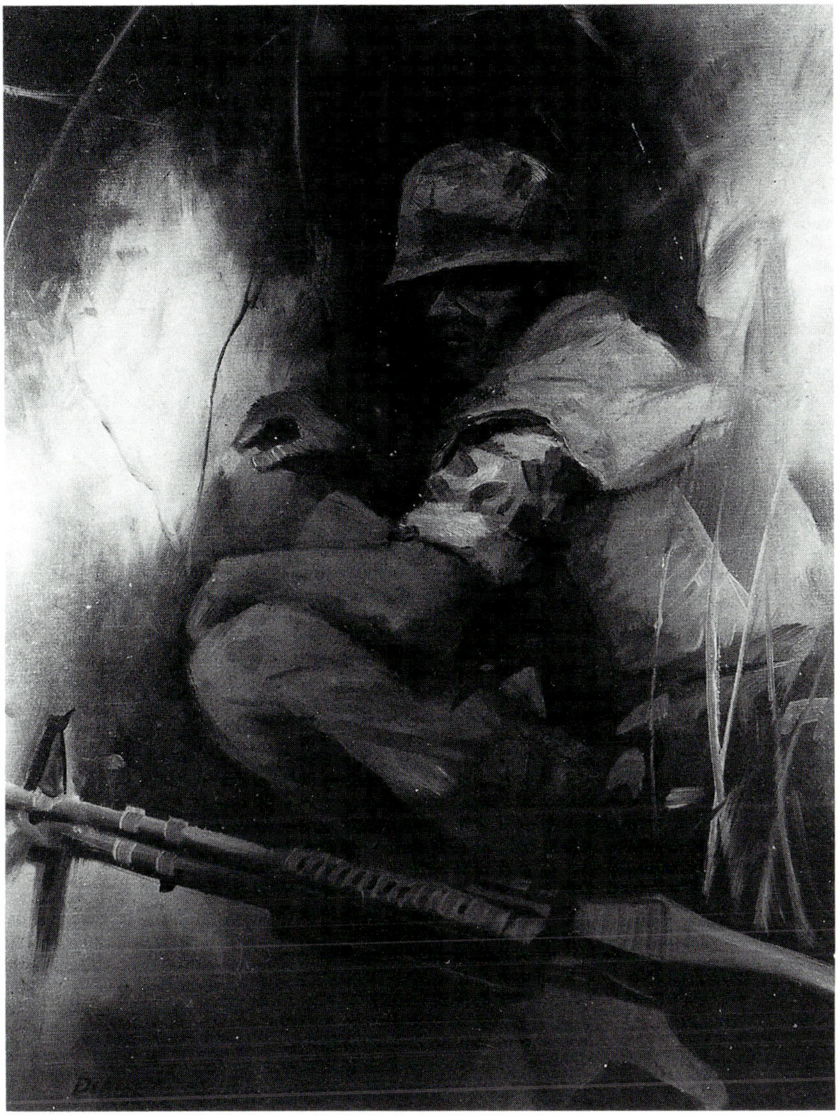

Once the attack began, the night would resemble a huge psychedelic light show, with tracers arcing through the darkness, flares gliding lazily down from the sky, steady streams of red tracers from circling "Puff" gunships and helicopter gunships, and above this Dante-like world, the distorted, static-ridden radios crackling out their frantic calls for help.

Men who had to stalk through the dark or had to lie in ambush could tell stories of fear-ridden minutes that seemed to stretch into eternity. Michael Herr vividly describes what going out at night meant to him:

Going out at night the medics gave you pills, Dexedrine breath like dead snakes kept too long in a jar. I never saw the need for them myself, a little contact or anything that even sounded like contact would give me more speed than I could bear. Whenever I heard something outside of our clenched little circle I'd practically flip, hoping to God that I wasn't the only one who noticed it. A couple of rounds fired off in the dark a kilometer away and the elephant would be there kneeling on my chest, sending me down into my boots for breath. Once I caught myself just under a whisper saying, "I'm not ready for this, I'm not ready for this."[22]

71. JAMES G. SCOTT
Incident, Ham Luong River 1969, Oil and acrylic, 24″ × 18″ (Navy Combat Art Coll.)

72. WALTER GIORDANO
Sunset in Xeo-Ro 1969, Oil
on canvas, 18″ × 26″ (U.S.
Navy Combat Art Coll.)

73. LEONARD H.
DERMOTT
Perimeter Wire 1967,
Watercolor (U.S. Marine Corps
Art Coll.)

77

74. LEONARD H. DERMOTT **Sweep** 1967, Watercolor, 18″ × 24″ (U.S. Marine Corps Art Coll.)

75. A. MICHAEL LEAHY **Close Air for INDIA** 1968, Felt-tip pen, 18″ × 24″ (U.S. Marine Corps Art Coll.)

Television and movies have led to the erroneous perception of battle as an orderly, logical progression. When the movie hero is receiving reports, for example, the radio is always clear and only one person is talking at a time. Compare that with the reality of any of the many recorded radio transmissions of an engagement, where it seems that a dozen people are talking at once, more than one radio is crackling, and other people are shouting for attention, and all the while there is an overriding cacophony of small arms, incoming mortar, and artillery shells. No combat artist or photographer has ever been able to depict this confusion and how people react to it. Former army officer Robert Santos remembers his first time under fire:

I got up and ran around yelling, "Move this machine gun over" and "Do this over there." I mean, all this noise was just going past me. I still didn't know what this noise was. *Ping.* Just a little weird, something new. I finally got back after running around, sat down next to the RTO [radio telephone operator], and he said, "What

76. JOHN D. KURTZ
Firefight at Thu Duc 1968,
Oil, 30″ × 40″ (U.S. Army
Center of Military Hist.)

77. BENJAMIN LONG IV **Snipers in Hedgerow** 1970, Pencil, 9″ × 12″ (U.S. Marine Corps Art Coll.)

78. HOWARD TERPNING **Moving Up** 1968, Acrylic, 18″ × 24″ (U.S. Marine Corps Art Coll.)

80

the fuck are you doing?" I said, "What do you mean?" He said,

the fuck are you doing?" I said, "What do you mean?" He said, "Don't you know what's going on?" I said, "Yeah, goddamnit. I know what's going on. Who do you think I am?" He says, "Don't you know what that noise is?" I said no. He said, "That's the bullets going over your head." I never knew. . . . if I'd known it I probably would've just buried myself and hid.[23]

NOTES

1. Clark Dougan, Stephen Wise, and the editors of Boston Publishing Company, *The American Experience in Vietnam* (New York: W. W. Norton, 1988), 165.
2. Don Oberdorfer, *Tet!* (Garden City, N.Y.: Doubleday, 1971), 201.
3. Quoted in Dougan et al., *American Experience in Vietnam*, 166.
4. Ibid.
5. Ibid.
6. Ibid., 176–177; Bernard C. Nalty, *Air Power and the Fight for Khe Sanh* (Washington, D.C.: Office of Air Force History, U.S. Air Force, 1973), 88.
7. John A. Cash, John Albright, and Allen W. Sandstrum, *Seven Firefights in Vietnam* (Washington, D.C.: Office of the Chief of Military History, U.S. Army, 1970), 112–119.
8. Ibid., 119.

79. STEPHEN H. SHELDON
Fire Coming In   1967, Pencil on paper, 11¾″ × 16¾″ (U.S. Army Center of Military Hist.)

9. Ibid., 129–130; Clark Dougan, Stephen Wise, and the editors of Boston Publishing Company, *Nineteen Sixty-Eight* (Boston: Boston Publishing Co., 1983), 48–49.

10. Dougan et al., *American Experience in Vietnam*, 177.

11. Michael Herr, *Dispatches* (New York: Alfred A. Knopf, 1977), 113.

12. Dougan et al., *American Experience in Vietnam*, 177.

13. Robert Pisnor, *The End of the Line: The Siege of Khe Sanh* (New York: W. W. Norton, 1982), 214.

14. Eric M. Hammel, *Khe Sanh: Siege in the Clouds. An Oral History* (New York: Crown, 1989), 245.

15. Pisnor, *End of the Line*, 210.

16. Ibid.

17. Dougan et al., *American Experience in Vietnam*, 120. See also Gary L. Telfer, Lane Rogers, and V. Keith Flemming, Jr., *U.S. Marines in Vietnam: Fighting the North Vietnamese, 1967* (Washington, D.C.: U.S. Marine Corps, 1984), 86–104.

18. Dougan et al., *American Experience in Vietnam*, 120; David Douglas Duncan, *War Without Heroes* (New York: Harper, 1970), 59–146.

19. Ibid., 106.

20. Dougan et al., *American Experience in Vietnam*, 120.

21. Kent Anderson, *Sympathy for the Devil* (Garden City, N.Y.: Doubleday, 1987), 311–312.

22. Herr, *Dispatches*, 4–5.

23. Al Santoli, *Everything We Had: An Oral History of the Vietnam War by Thirty-Three American Soldiers Who Fought It* (New York: Random House, 1981), 112–113.

80. JOHN STEEL
Wounded Marine Returns Fire 1967, Acrylic, 9½″ × 12¾″ (U.S. Navy Combat Art Coll.)

Chapter 6

SHATTERED BODIES,
SHATTERED MINDS

In this final chapter dealing with the world of the combat soldier, we see the last of the three areas in which the combat artists of the Vietnam War excel: the portrayal of compassion, togetherness, a sense of selflessness, and the final reckoning of war. There is no doubt that racism was present in the American military in Vietnam. In countless works of fiction and nonfiction, however, two constant themes are how any question of race seemed to be set aside and the sense of selflessness of the men in the bush. What seemed to matter was how one helped his fellow soldier. Nowhere is this more evident than when a grunt was wounded.

81. JOHN T. DYER, JR.
The Sniper 1968, Acrylic on masonite board (U.S. Marine Corps Art Coll.)

82. ISA BARNETT **Casualty** 1967, Felt-tip pen, 14″ × 15″ (U.S. Marine Corps Art Coll.)

83. HENRY C. CASSELLI, JR.
Man Against Time 1969, Mixed media, 30″ × 40″ (U.S. Marine Corps Art Coll.)

84. JOHN STEEL   **Chest Wound**   [n.d.], Acrylic, 8¼″ × 7″ (U.S. Navy Combat Art Coll.)

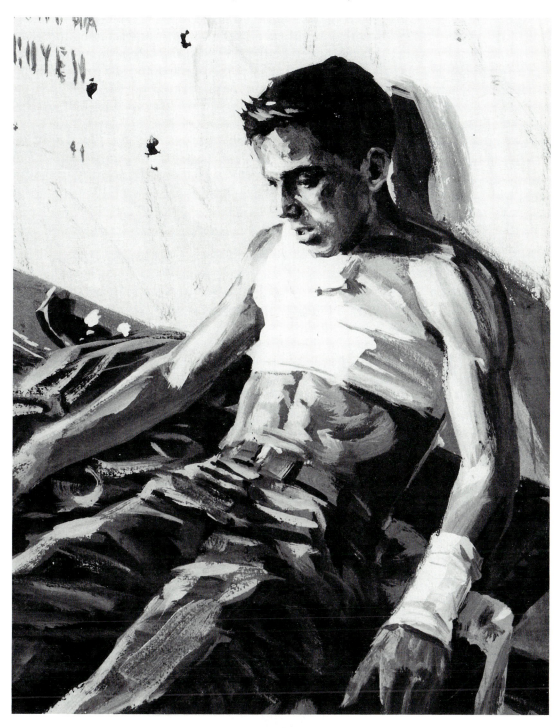

Writers have commented on the efforts made to get the wounded to medical help and on the amount of compassion shown by those in the bush toward those who were hurt. It is in the need to provide assistance and, mainly, in the feeling of compassion that the artists bring a dimension of understanding to the men in the field. After examining thousands of works of art on the Vietnam War, I believe Henry C. Casselli's *Corpsman* (Illus. 89) best represents the compassion felt by the soldiers in the bush. Read the citation (later in this chapter) for the Medal of Honor presented posthumously to Hospital Corpsman Third Class Wayne Marice Caron, and then reexamine Casselli's work. Look into the face of the marine in A. Michael Leahy's *The Cost Was High* (Illus. 97) to see the emotions registered by those who must face the death of their comrades. The work by Houston Stiff at the end of this chapter is the ultimate statement on the meaning of war. This chapter, therefore, will show the sense of togetherness, the selflessness, and the compassion of those who had to live with the constant chance of death. The reader should remember that while these men were caring for each other, they perceived that no one else cared about them. The really good artists of the war also caught this forgotten feeling in the faces of the soldiers.

85. HENRY C.
CASSELLI, JR.
Med-evac 1968, Pencil (U.S.
Marine Corps Art Coll.)

In the midst of a firefight, one man's duty is to save lives. In the U.S. Army that man is known as a combat medic, and in the U.S. Marine Corps he is a U.S. Navy combat corpsman. There is usually no love lost between sailors and marines, but on the subject of combat corpsmen it is a different story. Marine General Lewis K. Walt writes: "To the Marine infantryman undoubtedly the greatest guy going is the Navy corpsman attached to his platoon. He's the man on the spot ready to apply a band-aid to a blister or a tourniquet to a severed artery; and he's there no matter how grim or dangerous the situation gets."[1] Most corpsmen quickly became "Doc" to the marines.

Television and movies can try to depict combat, but nothing can prepare a person for the reality of war: wounds and death. Jack P. Smith, a former army infantryman pinned down under fire in the Ia Sanh Valley, wrote:

86. JOHN STEEL
Wounded Being Hoisted to Helicopter [n.d.], Acrylic, 10¼″ × 10¾″ (U.S. Navy Combat Art Coll.)

When a man is hit in the belly, he screams an unearthly scream. Something you cannot imagine; you actually have to hear it. . . . He keeps on screaming, sometimes until he dies. I just lay there, numb, listening to the bullets whining over me and the 15 or 20 men close to me screaming and screaming and screaming. They kept on until they were hoarse, then they would wake up and start screaming again. Then they would die. I started crying.[2]

Smith himself was wounded during the battle and was one of the few men in his battalion to survive.

It is under these intense periods of contact that "Doc" would rush out to help the wounded. Years after his service, Douglas Anderson, a former corpsman, recalled that he did not look upon himself as "a heroic type of individual. I don't

87. JOHN STEEL
Treating a Face Wound
[n.d.], Acrylic, 9½″ × 7¾″
(U.S. Navy Combat Art Coll.)

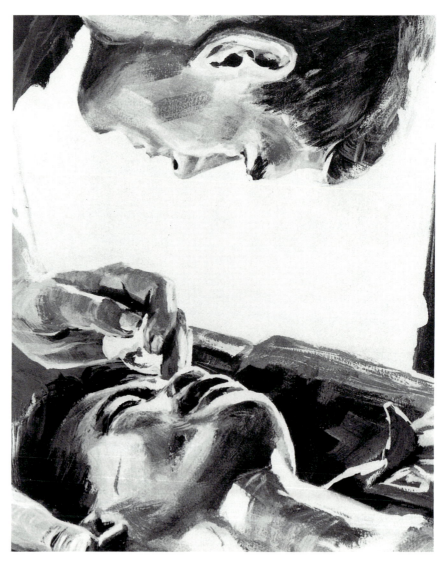

believe that I got up and ran under fire as much as I did to get to people. I don't believe I made myself do those things." Anderson then said of the marines he served with: "They knew if they got hit that I would come after them. . . . I know that if I had been hit and there was no way to get out of there, they would have grabbed me up in a poncho and carried me a hundred miles if they had to."[3]

Anderson's recollections bring out the trait that all combat veterans and thoughtful observers of the men in the bush have commented on: how the soldiers in the field cared for each other. Indeed, this seems to be a universal feeling among combat soldiers, for Eric Maria Remarque, in his classic 1929 antiwar novel, *All Quiet on the Western Front*, notes that the best thing to come out of the war was comradeship.

88. JOHN STEEL
Plasma Aboard
Helo [n.d.], Acrylic, 9″ × 8″
(U.S. Navy Combat Art Coll.)

In novel after novel, and in the reminiscences of veterans of the Southeast Asian conflict, the common thread that runs throughout is how little the color of one's skin or one's status mattered when in combat. Each man did his best to help the others. If wounded, the soldier *knew* that his buddies would do everything possible to get him to a medical evacuation helicopter, a "dust off." Medal of Honor winner Sam Davis recalled:

No one who served there [in combat] could escape or endure the terror, the heat, or the tremendous physical demands made by the war simply by applying himself to the task. Most of what carried us through the experience came out of the sense that everyone needed everyone else, that if you helped me today I would help you tomorrow. We would both help a third the next day. . . . We all looked out for each other.[4]

I can think of no single piece of combat art that better expresses this feeling among those who fought in Vietnam than Casselli's *Corpsman* (Illus. 89). The corpsman anxiously scans the sky for a dust-off as he holds and tries to bring a measure of solace to a wounded marine. Casselli's drawing brings out the compassion of the combat soldier for his fellow soldier and all of the fear and agony of those facing the very real chance of painful wounds or death. One should recall that while the emotions of fear, anxiety, and many others were going through the men in the field, they knew that outside of their immediate world in Vietnam, no one really cared.

Once again, Michael Herr has deftly cut to the core of the difficulties those on the homefront had in trying to understand what was happening in Vietnam. In general, the media, and the veterans themselves, reported on the brutality that went hand in hand with the war. The confused homefront then began to transfer its natural revulsion against real and alleged atrocities to every grunt in the field. Herr writes:

Disgust doesn't begin to describe what they made me feel, they threw people out of helicopters, tied people up and put the dogs on them. Brutality was just a word in my mouth before that. But disgust was only one color in the whole mandala, gentleness and pity were other colors, there wasn't a color left out. I think those people who used to say they only wept for the Vietnamese never really wept for anyone at all if they couldn't squeeze out at least one for these men and boys when they died or had their lives cracked open for them.[5]

The following is the citation for the award of the Congressional Medal of Honor to Hospital Corpsman Third Class Wayne Marice Caron, U.S. Navy:

While on a sweep through an open rice field in Quang Nam Province, Petty Officer Caron's unit started receiving enemy small-arms fire. Upon seeing two Marine casualties fall, he immediately ran forward to render first aid, but found that they were dead. At this time, the platoon was taken under intense small-arms and automatic-weapons fire, sustaining additional casualties. As he moved to the aid of his comrades, . . . Caron was hit in the arm by enemy fire. Although knocked to the ground, he regained his feet and continued to the injured Marines. He rendered medical assistance to the first Marine he reached, who was grievously wounded, and undoubtedly was instrumental in saving the man's life. . . . Caron then ran toward the second Marine, but was again hit by enemy fire, this time in the leg. Nonetheless, he crawled the remaining distance and provided medical aid for this severely wounded man. . . . Caron started to make his way to yet another injured comrade, when he was again struck by enemy small-arms fire. Courageously and with unbelievable determination, . . . Caron continued his attempt to reach the third Marine until he himself was killed by an enemy rocket round.[6]

89. HENRY C. CASSELLI, JR. **Corpsman** 1968, Pencil, 22″ × 28″ (U.S. Marine Corps Art Coll.)

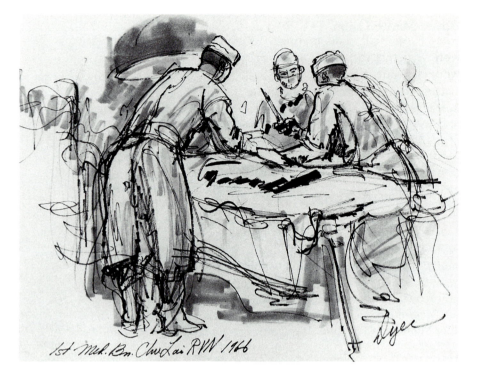

90. JOHN T. DYER, JR.   **Operation II**   1966, Mixed media (U.S. Marine Corps Art Coll.)

91. ROBERT ARNOLD   **Trying to Stop Blood**   1968, Felt-tip pen, 9″ × 12″ (U.S. Marine Corps Art Coll.)

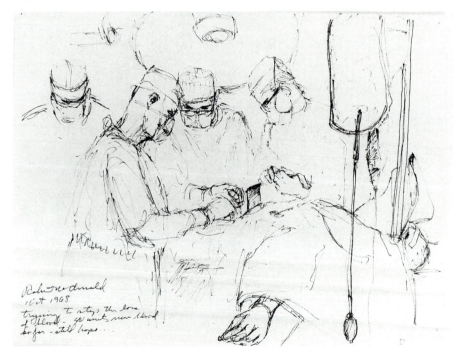

The emotions of the soldiers come through in the works depicting the aftermath of battle. Casselli's *Afterwards* (Illus. 96) shows a dazed marine in the rubble of a building wondering what happened. The marine's face in A. Michael Leahy's work registers the price paid by those who confront war and wonder about the cost. With a few exceptions, most combat artists did not show the actual wounding of men. Dyer's *The Sniper* (Illus. 81) one of the exceptions, is based on an actual observation near the DMZ. Dyer and Fairfax show the intense efforts of doctors. Casselli, again, renders the emotions of those who learn that their friends did not survive.

James Jones, in his narrative accompanying the combat art of World War II, is adamant about combat artists not showing the terrible things that bullets, shrapnel, and high explosives can do to a human body. Jones' observation can apply equally to the artists of the Vietnam War. However, one should ask, Is it really necessary actually to show the mangled, burned, and bloody bodies to bring home the ultimate agony of war? Houston Stiff's work *Dead at Khe Sanh Air Strip* (Illus. 99) is

92. JAMES A. FAIRFAX
The Surgeon 1969, Acrylic, 23″ × 29″ (U.S. Marine Corps Art Coll.)

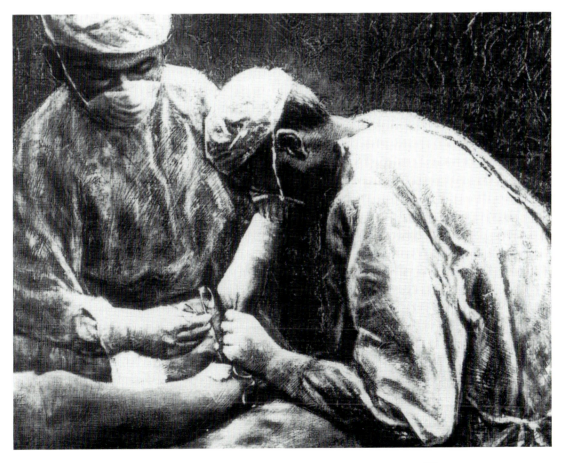

93. JOHN T. DYER, JR. **Aboard the Repose** 1966, Pen and ink (U.S. Marine Corps Art Coll.)

more evocative than dozens of grisly photographs showing bodies strewn about a field. In short, the emotions and eye of the artist can provide us with all of the horror of death without resorting to the shock value that some movie-makers seem to find necessary in their productions depicting war.

And who are the young men we are asking to go into action against such solid odds? You know. They are the best we have. But they are not McNamara's sons, or Bundy's. I doubt if they're yours. And they know they're at the end of the pipeline. That no one cares. They know.
    —An anonymous general to correspondent Arthur Hadley[7]

Night was near when two great birds beat through the clouds to squat upon the runway—two gaping-beaked, potbellied prehistoric birds: messengers come now to carry off the fallen men of that day's battle. Men joining those other men killed in all other wars. Then they were gone.
  And it was night.

—David Douglas Duncan,
War Without Heroes, 248

94. JOHN D. KURTZ
Intensive Care 1967, Oil, 32″ × 40″ (U.S. Army Center of Military Hist.)

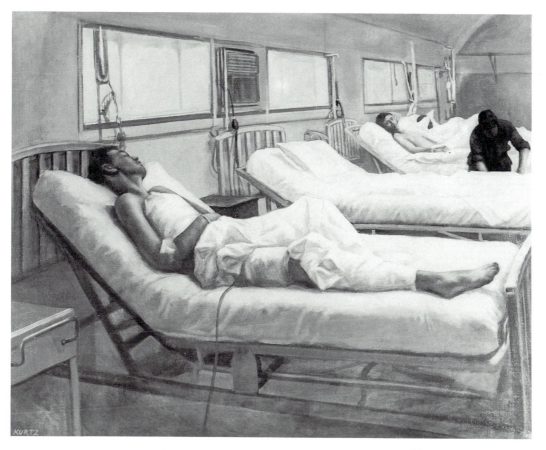

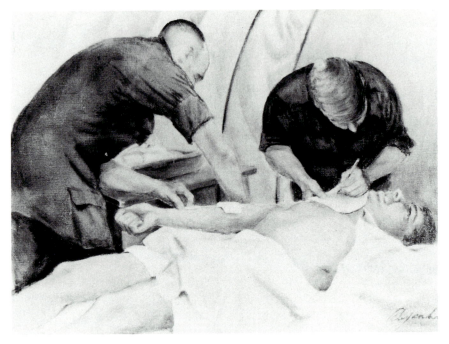

95. SAMUEL E. ALEXANDER **Next of Kin?** 1967, Oil on canvas, 20″ × 28″ (U.S. Army Center of Military Hist.)

96. HENRY C. CASSELLI, JR. **Afterwards** 1968, Pencil, 18″ × 25″ (U.S. Marine Corps Art Coll.)

97. A. MICHAEL LEAHY **The Cost Was High** 1967, Watercolor (U.S. Marine Corps Art Coll.)

98. HENRY C. CASSELLI, JR. **Death of a Friend** 1969, Acrylic, 20″ × 30″ (U.S. Marine Corps Art Coll.)

NOTES

1. Quoted in Edwin Bickford Hooper, *Mobility, Support, Endurance: A Study of Naval Operational Logistics in the Vietnam War, 1965–1968* (Washington, D.C.: Naval History Division, 1972), xi.

2. Harry G. Summers, Jr., "The Bitter Triumph of Ia Drang," *American Heritage* 35, no. 2 (February/March 1984), 57.

3. Al Santoli, *Everything We Had: An Oral History of the Vietnam War by Thirty-Three American Soldiers Who Fought It* (New York: Random House, 1981), 68, 75.

4. Clark Dougan, Stephen Wise, and the editors of Boston Publishing Company, *The American Experience in Vietnam* (New York: W. W. Norton, 1988), 119.

5. Michael Herr, *Dispatches* (New York: Alfred A. Knopf, 1977), 66.

6. U.S. Congress, Senate, *Medal of Honor Recipients, 1863–1978* (Committee on Veterans' Affairs, Senate Committee Print No. 3, 96th Congress, 1st Session, February 14, 1979), 818.

7. Quoted in James Webb, *Fields of Fire* (Englewood Cliffs, N.J.: Prentice-Hall, 1978), 1.

99. HOUSTON STIFF
Dead at Khe Sanh Air Strip   1968, Colored ink (U.S. Marine Corps Art Coll.)

Chapter 7

HUEYS, PHANTOMS, AND BROWN WATER: THE MACHINES OF WAR

The combat artists of the Vietnam War also covered those activities that represented the technological aspects of the war, with one exception. In this chapter the word *technology* will be used to denote all the large machines of war, such as tanks, helicopters, and naval craft. In general, most artists did not depict the electronics aspect of the war. One reason for this omission was that the equipment was classified.

Some of the works on the machines of war are masterful. Keith Ferris' *MIG Sweep* (Illus. 106), for example, places the viewer as close as possible to air-to-air combat without actually being in a jet fighter. R. G. Smith's *Launch* (Illus. 122) creates all of the power needed to hurl a jet aircraft from a carrier; while John Charles Roach's depiction of the battleship *New Jersey* (Illus. 124) ought to please any aficionado of these capital ships from another era. The irony of conducting a technological war in a nation that was basically rural was not lost on the artists. Douglas Rosa's and John Groth's works graphically point out this dichotomy. Lastly, even though this chapter focuses on the machines of war, there is also a human element brought out by the artists. Look at the faces of the deck crews on the aircraft carriers to see what it takes to put jets into the air. Maxine McCaffrey's *One Thunderchief Not Returning Today* (Illus. 107) gives the viewer the feeling of loss as a ground crew waits in vain for the return of their pilot and aircraft.

Throughout the course of the Vietnam War a debate raged among both military and civilian leaders over whether the war should be fought with the high technology available to the American military or by engaging in small-scale or guerrilla actions. This is not the place to cover that still ongoing debate. Suffice it to say, as with most issues dealing with the war,

99

that advocates for either side have presented their arguments with verve and passion. No matter which viewpoint one cares to take, there is little doubt that technology played a large part in the conflict. Electronic "people sniffers" dropped from aircraft could remotely transmit signals of footsteps in the jungle or could detect urine. Other sophisticated devices could intercept radio signals. Combat artists dealt extensively with the two machines of technology that for the general public have come most to symbolize the Vietnam War: the helicopter and the jet.

The helicopter has become the most recognized symbol of the war. It transported troops into battle and flew them quickly to medical help. It is not pushing the analogy too far to say that the helicopter became to the Vietnam War what the jeep was to World War II. The helicopter came in various sizes, from the small OH–13 "Loach" scout type to the huge HH–53 "Super Jolly Green Giant." But the machine most recognized by the average American is the UH–1 ("Huey").[1] A

100. EDWARD M. CONDRA III
Flight Line 1965, Felt-tip pen on paper, 18″ × 24″ (U.S. Marine Corps Art Coll.)

Huey could quickly ferry between six and eleven infantrymen into combat. The most indelible pictures of the war in the public's mind are the news films of a Huey coming into a landing zone, with heavily laden troops leaping out to engage the enemy. The distinctive pitch of the machine's rotors is a sound never to be forgotten by those who have heard it. The movie *Apocalypse Now* opens with the sounds of a Huey. This is inspired, for the sound has become so identified in our minds with the war that the audience knows immediately, without other sound effects such as gunfire, that this film will deal with Vietnam.

101. HOUSTON STIFF **Gunship Gunner** 1968, Acrylic, 16″ × 20″ (U.S. Marine Corps Art Coll.)

The other aerial weapon easily identified with the Vietnam War is the jet. Film on the six o'clock evening television news of jet aircraft screaming out of the sky to drop bombs in support of troops under fire became almost as common as watching Hueys disgorging troops. The graphic pictures of what napalm (jellied gasoline) did to humans, however, proved to be a very strong exhibit in the efforts of the antiwar movement to stop U.S. involvement in Vietnam.

The use of jet aircraft for bombing and close air support is well known. What many Americans may not realize about the air war is that some pilots were engaged in air-to-air combat with Soviet-supplied MiG 17s, 19s, and 21s while attacking targets in North Vietnam. Because of the high speeds involved, the engagements usually lasted only a few minutes, with most aircraft using missiles to make their kills. Keith Ferris' *MIG Sweep* (Illus. 106) gives the best representation of air-to-air combat in the skies over North Vietnam. We see the Phantom pilot maneuvering his aircraft to get onto the tail

102. A. MICHAEL LEAHY
Carlson's Raiders '67
1967, Watercolor on paper
(U.S. Marine Corps Art Coll.)

(the six-o'clock position) of the MiG, while attempting to sight the other aircraft, dimly visible far below to the left.

On May 20, 1967, U.S. Air Force pilots underwent an engagement that was unlike the typical scene depicted by Ferris. Two flights of F–4 Phantoms were escorting an F–105 Thunderchief strike force attacking the Bac Le railroad yards, southeast of the capital of North Vietnam, Hanoi, and the port city of Haiphong. The force came in from the west from the Gulf of Tonkin. The F–105s were to divide and strike two targets at the railroad yards, with a Phantom flight to cover each attack division. The attackers were taken under fire by surface-to-air missiles (SAMs), which were quickly suppressed. At nearly the same time, MiGs were reported. Fifteen miles short of the target, the first division of F–4s sighted MiGs. The other flight of Phantoms spotted more MiGs. Over the next twelve to fourteen minutes, according to the air force's official history of air-to-air combat in Vietnam, "there was a massive and aggressive dogfight with 8 F–4's battling 12–14 MIG–17's."[2] As the Phantoms engaged the MiGs, the F–105s continued on to their targets.

One participant in this "massive and aggressive dogfight" was Col. Robin Olds, along with his pilot, 1LT Stephen B.

103. LARRY ZABEL **Secondaries at Khe Sanh** 1968, Oil on aluminum, 24″ × 30″ (U.S. Navy Combat Art Coll.)

Croker. Olds, commander of the 8th Tactical Fighter Wing and a fighter ace during World War II, later remarked that the fight was "quite a remarkable air battle." Olds went on to report:

We were in our escort position, coming in from the Gulf of Tonkin. We just cleared the last of the low hills lying north of Haiphong, in an east-west direction, when about 10 or 12 MIG–17's came in low from the left and, I believe, from the right. They tried to attack the F–105's before they got to the target.

We engaged the MIG–17's approximately 15 miles short of the target. The ensuing battle was an exact replica of the dogfights of World War II.

Our flights of F–4's piled into the MIG's like a sledge hammer, and for about a minute and a half or two minutes that was the most confused, vicious dogfight I have been in. There were eight F–4C's, twelve MIG–17's, and one odd flight of F–105's on their way out from the target, who flashed through the battle area.

Quite frankly, there was not only danger from the guns of the MIG's, but the ever-present danger of a collision to contend with. We went round and round that day with the battles lasting 12 to 14 minutes, which is a long time. This particular day we found that the MIG's went into a defensive battle down low, about 500 to 1,000

104. LARRY ZABEL
Napalm Along the Buffer Strip 1968, Oil on metal, 16¾" × 26¾" (U.S. Navy Combat Art Coll.)

feet. In the middle of this circle, there were two or three MIG's circling about a hundred feet—sort of in figure-eight patterns. The MIG's were in small groups of two, three, and sometimes four in a very wide circle. Each time we went in to engage one of these groups, a group on the opposite side of the circle would go full power, pull across the circle, and be in firing position on our tails almost before we could get into firing position with our missiles. This is very distressing, to say the least.

The first MIG I lined up was in a gentle left turn, range about 7,000 feet. My pilot achieved a boresight lock-on, went full system, narrow gate, interlocks in. One of the two Sparrows [missiles] fired in ripple guided true and exploded near the MIG. My pilot saw the MIG erupt in flame and go down to the left.

We attacked again and again, trying to break up that defensive wheel. Finally, once again, fuel considerations necessitated departure. As I left the area by myself, I saw that lone MIG still circling and so I ran out about ten miles and said that even if I ran out of fuel, he is going to know he was in a fight. I got down on the deck, about 50 feet, and headed right for him. I don't think he saw me for quite a while. But when he did, he went mad, twisting, turning, dodging and trying to get away. I kept my speed down so I wouldn't overrun him and I stayed behind him. He headed up a narrow little valley to a low ridge of hills. I knew he was either going to hit that ridge up ahead or pop over the ridge to save himself. The minute he popped over I was going to get him with a Sidewinder [missile].

I fired one AIM–9 [missile] which did not track and the MIG pulled over a ridge, turned left, and gave me a dead astern shot. I obtained a good growl [audio signal to fire]. I fired from about 25

105. KEITH FERRIS
Doumer Bridge 1977, Oil, 48″ × 72″ (U.S. Air Force Art Coll.)

106. KEITH FERRIS **MIG Sweep** 1976, Oil, 29″ × 40″ (U.S. Air Force Art Coll.)

to 50 feet off the grass and he was clear of the ridge by only another 50 to 100 feet when the Sidewinder caught him.

The missile tracked and exploded 5 to 10 feet to the right side of the aft fuselage. The MIG spewed pieces and broke hard left and down from about 200 feet.

I overshot and lost sight of him. I was quite out of fuel and all out of missiles and pretty deep in enemy territory all by myself, so it was high time to leave. We learned quite a bit from this fight. We learned you don't pile into these fellows with eight airplanes all at once. You are only a detriment to yourself.

Pilots who flew fighter-bomber missions against targets in North Vietnam also faced heavy anti-aircraft fire and SAMs. Ferris spent four months' time in research in order to produce his *Doumer Bridge* (Illus. 105). The results give us the best understanding, without actually being there, of the type of opposition some navy, air force, and marine pilots faced in these attacks.

Another weapon from the air mated an aircraft from another era with contemporary technology. An Air Force AC–47, the military version of the civilian DC–3 that first flew in the 1930s, was fitted with three electronic Gatling guns. The AC–47 gunships could spend longer hours in the air than a jet, and at lower speeds, thus providing a perfect craft for ground support. Each Gatling gun could spew out some 6,000 rounds

107. MAXINE McCAFFREY
One Thunderchief Not Returning Today 1967, Acrylic, 23″ × 35″ (U.S. Air Force Art Coll.)

per minute. Every fifth round was a tracer (a round illuminated by phosphorus) to correct the aim of the weapon. When seen at night the frequent tracers emerging from the weapon appeared to be a rain of fire from heaven. The aircraft also carried flares to help illuminate the target. The ships became known to the troops as "Spooky" or "Puff the Magic Dragon."[3] John T. Dyer, Jr.'s *Puff the Magic Dragon* (Illus. 109) graphically shows how apt the troops' name for this weapon was. Dyer's work does appear to depict a dragon's fiery breath lashing the ground. To realize the effect of this aerial weapon, one has only to listen to the hectic recorded radio calls for help from an isolated camp and then listen to the reports of how quickly "Puff" could break the back of the assault, even though the enemy might be in the wires of a camp.

Even though noted civilian authors, such as Bernard Fall, as well as some military officers, argued that the Vietnam War was a revolutionary one or a classic case of guerrilla warfare, the U.S. Army and Marine Corps still used some of the highly

108. GEORGE AKIMOTO
**AC–47 Spooky Mission
Near Saigon** 1969, Acrylic, 22″ × 28″ (U.S. Air Force Art Coll.)

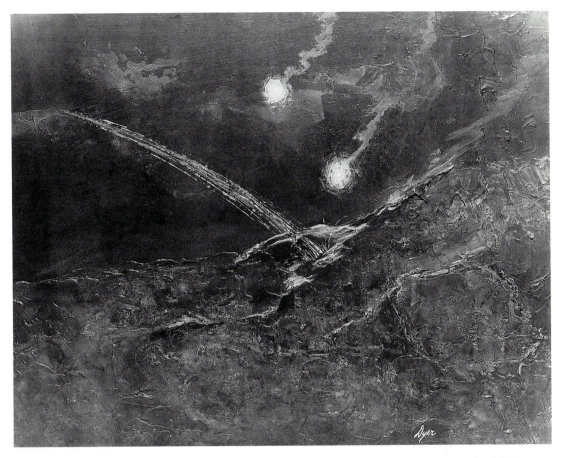

109. JOHN T. DYER, JR. **Puff the Magic Dragon** 1969, Acrylic, 22″ × 28″ (U.S. Marine Corps Art Coll.)

110. LEONARD H. DERMOTT **Falcon** 1967, Watercolor, 22″ × 28″ (U.S. Marine Corps Art Coll.)

109

111. LEONARD H. DERMOTT **ONTOS** 1967, Watercolor, 18″ × 22″ (U.S. Marine Corps Art Coll.)

112. MICHAEL R. CROOK **Vigil on the DMZ** 1967, Acrylic, 28″ × 40″ (U.S. Army Center of Military Hist.)

110

113. DOUGLAS ROSA **Buffalos and Helicopters** 1967, Acrylic, 18″ × 24″ (U.S. Marine Corps Art Coll.)

114. JOHN GROTH **Tanks and Girls** 1967, Watercolor (U.S. Marine Corps Art Coll.)

111

115. JOHN CHARLES ROACH **Phantom and Bombs on Deck** 1969, Pencil, 11″ × 13½″ (U.S. Navy Combat Art Coll.)

116. JOHN CHARLES ROACH **Squall Line** 1969, Oil on canvas, 28¾″ × 39½″ (U.S. Navy Combat Art Coll.)

mechanized equipment that may have been better suited for engagements with an enemy on different terrain. Tanks, APCs (armored personnel carriers), and other machines lumbered like prehistoric animals through the countryside. The use of these and other high-technology weapons among peasants working in rice fields is captured by Douglas Rosa's *Buffalos and Helicopters* (Illus. 113), while John Groth, in *Tanks and Girls* (Illus. 114), captures the sight of women peddling past marines aboard tanks.

Most media coverage of the naval war in Vietnam centered on the large ships of the U.S. Navy. Television news viewers were regularly shown scenes of aircraft carriers launching aircraft, while other surface ships provided shore bombardment with their large guns. It is easy to understand why carriers would receive the lion's share of film: the launching and recovery of jets aboard these large ships is an exciting activity to watch and one that is a natural visual image for the television viewer as a reporter discusses air strikes against Vietnam. While visually exciting, the work on a flight deck during aircraft

117. JOHN CHARLES ROACH
Bomb Loaders Sitting on Bombs 1969, Pencil, 11″ × 13½″ (U.S. Navy Combat Art Coll.)

operations is fatiguing and extremely dangerous. One former crewman whose duty was to hook planes to the catapult of the USS *Constellation* wrote:

Planes, men and tractors constantly flowed in a surrealistic dance of moving aircraft and potential death. One became adept at running under rapidly taxying aircraft, simultaneously dodging intakes, wheels and exhausts, all of which could kill very quickly. You learned to keep an eye on your work and the other on the lookout for a half-witted plane director about to make an aircraft either run over someone, or blow him off the deck.

I wore a plastic and canvas helmet designed to protect the wearer from small flying objects and to deaden the sound (an F–4 on afterburner is painful at 100 feet; we routinely stood 10 to 15 feet from them). Other items of equipment included goggles, leather gloves, steel-tipped shoes, and a life preserver in case one was blown overboard. The launchings had looked impressive from the island [the superstructure of the carrier]; however, at a few feet their power was impressive.[4]

118. JOHN CHARLES ROACH
Ordnance People with Bombs 1969, Pencil, 11″ × 13½″ (U.S. Navy Combat Art Coll.)

R. G. Smith's *Launch* (Illus. 122) captures the moment before a jet is hurled off the carrier's deck, while John Steel depicts a jet just prior to engaging the arresting wire and bringing it to a jarring halt. Look closely at the studies of the deck crewmen by John Charles Roach to see the fatigue of sailors engaged in aircraft operations aboard an aircraft carrier.

Modern naval warfare has given sailors the reputation of not having to engage the enemy up close. After all, a 74,000-ton carrier's main weapons are its aircraft, and it is unlikely to go alongside another ship to fight. Modern naval weaponry also allows other surface ships to work at long distances. The cruiser *Newport News*, for example, on May 10, 1972, arrived off the coast of North Vietnam and fired on targets near Haiphong. Each of her 335-pound, eight-inch projectiles sought out targets up to fourteen miles away. After twenty minutes of bombardment, and expending seventy-seven eight-inch shells and forty five-inch shells, she steamed away from the coast. In short, by the 1960s the days of naval combat where one actually saw the enemy seemed to have gone the way of cutlasses, muskets, and boarding parties. In one phase of the

119. JOHN CHARLES ROACH
Loading Bombs Under Wing with Ribbon 1969, Pencil, 11″ × 14″ (U.S. Navy Combat Art Coll.)

120. JOHN CHARLES ROACH **Flight Crew in Cockpit** 1969, Pencil, 13″ × 11″ (U.S. Navy Combat Art Coll.)

121. JOHN CHARLES ROACH **Phantom Ready for Launch** 1969, Pencil (U.S. Navy Combat Art Coll.)

Vietnam naval war, however, sailors once again engaged in old-fashioned, close-up combat. The men who fought in this little-known aspect of the war were overlooked by the media at the time and largely forgotten in the numerous books later published on the war.

A glance at a map of what was once South Vietnam reveals a long coastline and a network of rivers. The river systems provided both natural passageways through the country and obstacles for advancing troops. A long coastline invited the introduction of materiel to the Viet Cong. As will be brought out later, the contraband arriving in South Vietnam in the early 1960s was usually landed from small craft, junks, or trawlers capable of entering shallow waters. The river systems and long coastline caused a problem for the navy. The battleship *New Jersey* obviously could not sail up a shallow river, nor could she work close to the beach to interdict the large amount of shallow water coastal traffic. Very early in the U.S. involvement in South Vietnam, commanders felt that the problems presented by the rivers and shallow water coastal areas needed to be addressed. The solutions led to coastal and riverine warfare. The forgotten forces participating in this

122. R. G. SMITH
Launch 1969, Oil on canvas, 20″ × 20″ (U.S. Navy Combat Art Coll.)

aspect of the Vietnam War became known as the "Brown Water Navy."

The first obstacle facing the Brown Water Navy was a lack of craft capable of operating in shallow water and having the high performance necessary quickly to overtake suspect vessels. The only craft in the navy's inventory, prior to 1965, capable of operating in shallow water were amphibious landing craft, normally used in transporting troops or equipment from transport ships to an enemy beachhead. Most of these small craft drew very little water and were not armored, nor were they designed for the sustained offshore operations that would be required to interrupt any supplies coming in from the sea. The landing craft, therefore, were assigned to the rivers.

The use of amphibious craft on the rivers of South Vietnam began during the French period of the Indochina War. In 1945 Gen. Philippe Leclerc, commander of the French military forces in Indochina, ordered the establishment of a flotilla to operate in the Mekong Delta. The force would transport naval

123. JOHN STEEL
Wheels Down—Hook Down
1967, Acrylic, 7¾″ × 9½″
(U.S. Navy Combat Art Coll.)

infantrymen to locations where they were most needed. This force was known as the Naval Infantry River Flotilla; as its use was increased and more flotillas were added, the name was changed to *Divisions navales d'assaut* (naval assault divisions) and abbreviated to *Dinassauts*.[5]

The *Dinassauts* were ideal for the Mekong Delta, with its water-dominated terrain. In 1953 the Vietnamese Navy established two *Dinassauts* in the region, with two more activated just prior to the end of the French involvement in 1954. Eventually the numbers grew until there were seven *Dinassauts*. By the early 1960s the divisions became River Assault Groups, which Americans quickly abbreviated to RAG.

A River Assault Group usually consisted of nineteen craft, eleven of which were armored versions of LCVPs (landing craft, vehicle, personnel) and LCMs (landing craft, medium). These were used to transport the assault troops. Six craft were former French patrol boats. The remaining two vessels were a monitor and a *commandement*. Both of these boats were armored and were former LCMs. The monitor was designed for fire support and the *commandement* for communications. The Vietnamese Navy, however, relegated the groups to logistic support in the late 1950s and early 1960s. This was due

124. JOHN CHARLES ROACH
USS *New Jersey* off DaNang—Firing Inland   1969, Tempera, 20½″ × 28½″ (U.S. Navy Combat Art Coll.)

to the reliance upon American helicopters for transporting troops, which would change as the Americans entered the war.

In 1966 Gen. William C. Westmoreland began to consider committing more American troops to the Delta region of South Vietnam. The region is dominated by rice paddies and waterways and has only one major road (Route 4). In addition, the soil is so spongy that in many areas it is unable to support the weight of artillery. Troops traversing the area were quickly bogged down crossing the waterways or in the mud. The high temperatures and humidity reduced the lift of helicopters. What made the region important to the Viet Cong were the provinces of Dinh Tuong and Kien Hoa. These two provinces, which held most of the population in the Delta, were the key to the control of Route 4, the link between Saigon and the southeast, and the region was considered the "rice bowl" of South Vietnam.

One of the major problems in introducing American troops into the Delta was where to establish a base. Most of the land available was taken up by farming, and to build a base would mean pushing people off their farms, thus providing more propaganda material for the Viet Cong. General Westmoreland's answer to this was to adopt "an idea advanced originally by a U.S. Navy officer, Capt. David F. Welch. In much the

125. THEODORE J. ABRAHAM
Mobile Riverine Group 1967, Acrylic on board, 23⅞" × 19⅞" (U.S. Army Center of Military Hist.)

120

same way that U.S. forces in, for example, the Seminole War and the Civil War had used waterways to facilitate military operations, why could we not create special units equipped to utilize the extensive waterways of the Delta to get at the Viet Cong?"[6] This marks the beginning of the Mobile Riverine Force.

The U.S. Navy provided the craft that would transport infantry troops into combat operations. Normally, the troops would be U.S. Marines, but they were committed to the north-ernmost regions of South Vietnam. Instead, the army reacti-vated the Ninth Infantry Division, and the Second Brigade was to operate with the Mobile Riverine Force. The base for the troops when not in action comprised several converted LSTs (landing ship, tank) converted to barracks and repair vessels. To provide navy and army personnel with a shore base for relief from living aboard the LSTs, the Army Corps of Engineers and the navy's Seabees dredged sand from the bottom of the My Tho River. General Westmoreland named the newly created land area Dong Tam—"united hearts and minds."

The small craft engaged in actual combat operations were organized into River Assault Flotilla I in September 1966 and consisted of two river assault squadrons and one river support squadron. Most of the assault craft were much like the earlier French boats, but more heavily armed and with better armor. There were some unusual modifications. Small landing pads were fashioned for helicopters, thus allowing for the evacua-tion of casualties. Some assault craft were converted into small "hospital ships," which could treat up to fifty-six wounded. Finally, some craft were equipped with fuel bladders to create "oilers" for refueling. Barges, towed by LCMs, carried 105-mm howitzers for artillery support. In 1968 the Mobile Riv-erine Force was expanded to include two additional squad-rons. In February 1969 some boats began to be turned over to the South Vietnamese Navy, which continued until the force was dissolved in August 1969.[7]

Of all the units operating within the Brown Water Navy, the Mobile Riverine Force received the most attention, no doubt because its mission was to transport and land infantry troops to engage and destroy the enemy. Other aspects of the naval forces operating on South Vietnam's waterways or coastal areas, such as Operation Market Time and Game Warden (discussed below), dealt with the cutting off of supplies. This is not to imply, however, that the soldiers and sailors in this force were constantly in the headlines. They too failed to receive their share of recognition. Soldiers who spent more than three days in the field often suffered from "immersion foot," caused by long periods of time slogging through water. The soldiers of the riverine force exhibited much bravery.

On the night of November 17, 1967, C Battery, 2nd Battalion, 4th Artillery, located near My Tho on the Mekong River, came under heavy mortar attack at two in the morning, followed by a massed attack by North Vietnamese Army troops across the Mekong River. Twenty-one-year-old Pfc. Sammy L. Davis, an assistant gunner, lowered his tube and began firing his 105-mm gun directly at the advancing troops.[8] Davis' gun shield received a direct hit from a rocket-propelled grenade. "I got thousands of little . . . pieces of steel in my right side and was knocked unconscious," Davis later recalled. The remaining crew gathered up all the men they thought were alive and fell back to the next artillery piece, believing that Davis was among the dead.

Davis recovered consciousness when hit by some flechettes (dartlike projectiles contained within some artillery rounds) from U.S. weapons and "realized what I had to do." The artilleryman began to fire his M16 until it quit, then he found an M60 machine gun and fired that until it quit, and still "they just kept coming." Davis felt that the only thing left was to see if he could get a 105-mm artillery piece and fire it himself. Later, quite matter-of-factly, the young soldier stated, "So that's what I did."

The recoil mechanism in the tube that Davis fired was damaged, and the entire artillery piece would jump backward. "Every time I fired it, it just kept jumping back and back." The weapon rolled over Davis and broke some vertebrae in his back. "If it hadn't been for the soft mud, it probably would have killed me." Still, Davis kept up his fire, with the piece ending up in a creek about eight feet away from the original position. "I had to load the last round underwater, but it went off." Davis' fire kept one flank from being overrun.

Davis then noticed a wounded soldier across the river. Knowing he was hurt too badly to help the man by himself, he found an air mattress and somehow worked his way across the river. Upon reaching the wounded soldier, Davis found two more men. One man was hit in the back, another in the head, and the third in the foot. Davis, with almost superhuman strength, "threw the guy . . . shot in the head over my back," and had the other two lean on each shoulder. "We all kind of leaned on each other and helped each other back toward the river." As the four men were struggling toward the water, some NVA ran past the group but did not seem to notice. Davis got the man with the head wound across the river first and then went back for the remaining two. For his actions, Davis received the United States' highest military award, the Medal of Honor.[9]

Brown water sailors, as will be shown later, unlike their deep water shipmates, faced both small arms and mortar fire. In many cases, the sailors faced the same conditions as the infantry.

If the Brown Water Navy received very little attention on the homefront, then the role of the nation's smallest armed force, the U.S. Coast Guard, went almost completely unnoticed. In fact, many Americans may not realize that this service, most noted for rescues, had a combat role in Southeast Asia. Coast guardsmen performed a multitude of duties ranging from maintaining aids to navigation, to providing port security details, which supervised the loading and unloading of dangerous cargoes, to providing shipping advisors and merchant marine details to help merchant shipping. At least fifty-six combat cutters were assigned to Vietnamese waters to provide gunfire support missions. One of the largest missions undertaken by the U.S. Coast Guard, however, was the work accomplished by small eighty-two-foot patrol boats in Operation Market Time.[10]

By 1965 the United States was concerned about the infiltration of weapons into South Vietnam from the sea. The

126. NOEL DAGGETT
And They Call It Market Time 1970, Oil, 30" × 24"
(U.S. Coast Guard Art Coll.)

infiltration was accomplished in two ways: by coastwise junk traffic, which hid among the more than 50,000 registered civilian craft plying Vietnam's coastal waters; and by vessels of trawler size (usually steel-hulled), which sailed innocently in international waters and, at a given location, would make a perpendicular approach to the coast. The trawlers probably originated in North Vietnam and the People's Republic of China.

General Westmoreland, on March 3, 1965, called a conference to plan ways to stop the infiltration. It was decided that a conventional sea patrol be established by U.S. Navy ships and aircraft. A defensive area, extending forty miles out to sea, would be set, and American forces would stop, board, and search vessels in its waters and the contiguous zone. The work would come under the name Operation Market Time.

Market Time operations were divided into nine patrol areas, stretching from the 17th Parallel to the Brevie Line in the Gulf of Thailand. The Brevie Line is the geographic division in the Gulf of Thailand between Vietnam and Cambodia.

127. NOEL DAGGETT
A War of Persuasion 1970, Oil, 42″ × 40″ (U.S. Coast Guard Art Coll.)

124

Islands and territorial waters to the north of that line are Cambodian; those to the south are Vietnamese. Normally, a destroyer escort (radar) or an oceangoing minesweeper was responsible for each patrol area.

The need for shallow water craft to undertake this operation led the Secretary of the Navy, Paul Nitze, to request the Secretary of the Treasury, Henry H. Fowler, to inform him of the availability of U.S. Coast Guard units to deploy to Vietnam. At this time, the U.S. Coast Guard operated under the Treasury Department. On April 30, 1965, U.S. Coast Guard Squadron One, consisting of eighty-two-foot patrol boats, was formed.

The boat was ideal for Operation Market Time. The craft was designed to be operated by a small crew. For example, the machinery was designed to facilitate underway operations without a continuous engine room watch, and engine speed was controlled by throttles on the bridge. The bridge was designed so that all navigation equipment, radio, radar, and engine controls were centered on a console about the wheel. If necessary, one man could steer, control the speed, guard the radar, observe the fathometer, and operate the radio. This ability was especially useful when most of the crew was on deck during operations.

The patrol boat was twin-screwed, propelled by two turbocharged, 600-shaft horsepower VT–12M Cummings diesel engines, one on each shaft. The hull was constructed of black steel and had six watertight compartments. The superstructure was built of aluminum. The patrol boat displaced sixty-five tons and, most important, drew only six feet of water. Finally, she could berth and mess a crew for a short period of time. This craft was the only shallow water patrol boat that had this ability and thus could remain on patrol for longer periods of time.

The boats were modified for their combat role. A .50-caliber machine gun was mounted on top of an 81-mm mortar. This piggyback armament was then placed on the boat's bow. Four additional .50-caliber machine guns were installed on the main deck, aft the wheel-house. Ready service boxes were installed on deck to store the additional ammunition. Other changes ranged from better reefers to more bunks.

Initially, 47 officers and 198 enlisted men formed Coast Guard Squadron One. Before departing for Vietnam they received additional training in gunnery, communications, escape and evasion, and other military subjects. A total of seventeen boats made up the squadron. The first units arrived in Vietnam on July 20, 1965.

The cutters, as were all Market Time surface units, were expected to "conduct surveillance, gunfire support, visit and search, and other operations as directed along the coast of the Republic of Vietnam in order to assist the Republic of Vietnam in detection and prevention of Communist infiltration from the seas." When ready for a patrol, a cutter would report to the minesweeper or destroyer escort-maintaining outer-barrier patrol. The outer patrol would provide radar and navigation assistance to the cutter. In a like manner, the cutter would provide the same information to South Vietnamese Navy junk units working close to the beach. In the Gulf of Thailand, six of the nine patrol boats were constantly on patrol, each in one of six designated subareas. The boats were under way for four days, and then they returned to the support ship for two days. Each boat rotated through all the subareas.

Life on board the small patrol boats was hard, as the crew worked from twelve to sixteen hours a day when under way. In the Gulf of Thailand area, for instance, the boats had a three-section watch: three men—the officer-of-the deck, helmsman, and radioman—stood a four-hour watch; a second section served as a boarding party; the third would be off duty. The captain and cook stood no watches. An officer was on hand for all boardings. The men had to be on guard constantly, as any common fishing craft could suddenly open fire with automatic weapons. Eventually, most crew members learned the maxim: "Don't relax. It could mean your life!"

In the first month of patrols, the cutter crews boarded more than 1,100 junks and sampans, inspected more than 4,000 Vietnamese craft, and worked more than 4,800 man-hours. To counter the cutters' efforts, the Viet Cong told local fishermen that the U.S. boats were driving them from the best fishing grounds so that U.S. fishing boats could fish there. To counter this move, the U.S. Coast Guard, Navy, and South Vietnamese, developed an information program aimed at the fishermen, which included medical care.

By October 1965 it became apparent that Market Time forces were spread too thin, and nine additional cutters were deployed to Vietnam. This group, Division Thirteen, took station at Vung Tau in early 1966.

The year was a busy and dangerous one for the sailors of the small cutters. One representative action will be described. On May 10, 1966, the U.S. Coast Guard cutter *Point Grey* was patrolling the east side of the Ca Mau Peninsula when her crew spotted bonfires on the beach. While investigating the fires, the patrol boat picked up a steel-hulled target on her radar about six miles to seaward attempting to close the beach.

The contact was tentatively identified as a one-hundred-foot Chinese Nationalist vessel, traveling at a speed of 10 knots.

The *Point Grey* began to shadow the trawler. At 2:40 A.M. the trawler was within one mile of the beach opposite the fires, with three or four persons observed on deck. By 5:00 A.M. the contact was within one-half mile of the beach, and the *Point Grey*'s commanding officer notified his operational commander on the destroyer escort USS *Brewster* that he would board the trawler at daylight. Two hours later, the cutter closed the trawler. The craft was found aground and deserted. As the men of the *Point Grey* attempted to board the trawler, they came under fire from the beach. The cutter moved out of small arms range and began to lob 81-mm mortar rounds at the gun positions on the beach.

For the next six hours, the *Point Grey* kept the trawler under surveillance. At 1:30 P.M. without air or naval gunfire support, the cutter again closed the trawler. At about 200 yards from the beach and within 100 yards of the trawler, the cutter came under "extremely accurate small arms and automatic weapons fire." Within twenty to thirty seconds, three of the four men on the bow of the *Point Grey* were hit: a coast guardsman, a U.S. Army major, and the South Vietnamese Navy liaison officer.

The cutter took about twenty-five hits, but no one was seriously hurt. Air strikes were called in to suppress the fire. The *Point Grey*'s crew then boarded the vessel. The haul from the trawler proved impressive. Contraband, including an estimated fifty to sixty tons of arms, ammunition, and supplies, was confiscated.

On May 16, 1969, the U.S. Coast Guard began to transfer some of the cutters to the South Vietnamese Navy. By August 15, 1970, the last of the twenty-six cutters were transferred to the South Vietnamese Navy. This ended the role of the U.S. Coast Guard's eighty-two-foot patrol boats in Vietnam.

The statistics of U.S. Coast Guard Squadron One are impressive. The coast guard boarded 236,527 vessels, participated in 4,461 naval gunfire support missions, cruised 4,215,116 miles, damaged or destroyed 1,811 vessels, and wounded or killed 1,055 of the enemy. The U.S. Coast Guard casualties were seven killed and fifty-three wounded.

Noel Daggett's *A War of Persuasion* (Illus. 127) shows the cutter *Point Banks* and a navy Swift boat fighting their way up a river during Operation Market Time and is a good representation of how the two U.S. naval forces operated on the rivers of South Vietnam.

By the middle of the 1960s the naval forces in Vietnam had

the use of amphibious craft for the rivers and U.S. Coast Guard patrol boats for both rivers and coastal waters during Operation Market Time. What was still needed were small, fast boats that could quickly intercept suspected vessels. The first of these came on the scene during Market Time and had its genesis in the boats used to transport crews to oil rigs in the Gulf of Mexico. Seward Seacraft of Burwick, Louisiana, manufactured a fifty-foot, all-welded aluminum alloy boat and soon agreed to produce a version for the navy. The craft, which was officially designated a PCF (patrol craft, fast), became known to the Brown Water Navy as the "Swift boat." The snub-nosed boats were fifty feet in length, displaced nineteen tons, and had a draft of only three and a half feet. They had twin screws and were powered by two diesel engines, which could push them through the brown water at speeds up to 28 knots. The boats were armed with a twin .50-caliber machine gun located in a gun tub atop the pilothouse. A piggyback arrangement of mortar and machine gun similar to those aboard U.S. Coast Guard patrol boats was placed on the fantail of the Swift boats. The boats were also equipped with electronics, including radar.

Eighty-five boats were eventually deployed to South Vietnam, beginning in 1965, and were organized into five divisions, each commanded by a lieutenant (j.g.) with a crew of five enlisted men. The duties of these small boats on Market Time were, as depicted by Daggett, the same as those of the U.S. Coast Guard cutters.

Another important small craft developed for the Brown Water Navy was the PBR (patrol boat, river). The prototype for the boat was developed by Willis Slane, president and founder of the Hatteras Yacht Company. In 1965 Slane put water-jet pumps on a twenty-eight foot hull. The boat was able to make 30.5 knots with a range of 165 miles and drawing only nine inches of water. Here indeed was a fast boat for river warfare.

The boat the navy eventually accepted, however, was built by United Boatbuilders of Bellingham, Washington. It was thirty-one feet in length and had a fiberglass hull, twin General Motors 220-hp diesel engines, and no propellers. Instead, she had water-jet pumps that shot out a jet of water from nozzles located below the waterline on the stern to drive the boat through the water at high speeds. (The VC knew of this propulsion and sometimes floated cut weeds and grass into the water in advance of PBR patrols in an attempt to foul the jets.)

This dark-green craft weighed only 14,600 pounds and

could reverse course in her own length at full speed and stop dead in the water from full ahead within three lengths. Both of these features would give the crew a good soaking down. Ceramic armor, designed to stop bullets up to .30-caliber, covered the coxswain's flat and the weapons stations. At the bow was an open turret holding a twin .50-caliber machine gun. At the stern was a pedestal for a single machine gun. At each side, amidships, were mounts for either an M60 machine gun or an MK–18 grenade launcher. The boats were also equipped with electronic equipment, such as radios and radar.

The boats were noted for their speed, and speed was one of the survival factors for the crews of these craft. One must, however, put this factor into proper perspective. One salty chief petty officer was being interviewed by a reporter about the boat's almost legendary speed. The reporter noted that the boats "go like hell wide open." To which the chief replied: "They go twenty-five knots wide open. Ever try to outrun a cannon shell at twenty-five knots?"[11]

The PBR carried a crew of four, usually made up entirely of enlisted men. Boat captains ranged from second class petty officers to chief petty officers from all rates. The remainder of the crew was made up of an engineman, a gunner's mate,

128. GERALD MERFELD
Showing the Flag in Ca Mau 1969, Oil on canvas, 24″ × 36″ (U.S. Navy Combat Art Coll.)

and a seaman. All of the men were cross-trained in one another's duties so that any one of them could take over any position.

By 1965 there was a growing suspicion that the North Vietnamese were infiltrating supplies and men into the Mekong Delta from Cambodia. There was also concern over the Viet Cong's rising strength along the waterways leading to Saigon. In August 1965 the Secretary of Defense authorized the navy to wage riverine warfare in Vietnam. On December 13, 1965, a River Patrol Force was created under the name Operation Game Warden. The PBRs, of course, were the perfect craft for this type of work.

Operation Game Warden forces were to enforce curfews, interdict Viet Cong infiltration, prevent taxation of water traffic by the Viet Cong, and counter enemy movement and resupply efforts. In addition, the force was to keep the main shipping channel into Saigon open by patrolling and minesweeping in the Long Tau River.

The boats usually patrolled in pairs, which permitted one boat to cover the other. A chief petty officer or a junior officer usually served as patrol officer and was responsible for both boats. When available, a Vietnamese national policeman rode

129. R. G. SMITH
Fire Fight 1968, Oil on canvas, 20″ × 20″ (U.S. Navy Combat Art Coll.)

in the other craft, acting as liaison and interpreter.

Besides work that much resembled that of Market Time vessels, that is, boarding and searching suspect craft, the crews of the PBRs also set ambushes and provided transportation for SEAL (Sea, Air, Land) teams. But, in general, the work of Game Warden units centered on stopping logistical movements of the Viet Cong. However, this does not mean that the sailors did not see action. A case in point occurred during October 1966.

PBRs 105 and 99 were closing on two sampans loaded with troops in the middle of the My Tho River.[12] The troops were North Vietnamese regulars, an unusual sight at this time and place in South Vietnam. The two sampans split up, one heading for the north shore of the river, while the other took to the south. The PBRs engaged the southern craft and destroyed it. Boatswain's Mate First Class James Elliot Williams, boat captain of the 105 and patrol officer, ordered both PBRs in pursuit of the remaining sampan.

As the two boats raced at full throttle around a bend in a canal, they came upon an amazing sight. There in front of them were forty or fifty boats so ladened with troops that the sampans had about two inches of freeboard. Thomas J. Cutler writes that it "would be difficult to assess who was more startled, the crews of the PBRs upon suddenly finding the waterway full of an enemy 'fleet,' or the soldiers of the 261st and 262nd NVA regiments upon seeing these two patrol craft careening around the bend and hurtling down on them."

The PBRs opened fire, and the soldiers from the sampans began to return fire. The riverbanks began to erupt in small arms fire and the explosions of mortars. Williams, with little room to maneuver in, decided to press the attack. The 105 actually ran over the first sampan, followed by two others. Automatic weapons, rifle fire, and recoilless rifle fire all filled the air, with the North Vietnamese on shore probably hitting more of their own men. One recoilless rifle round actually went clear through the bow of the 105, exploding on the opposite bank among the NVA troops.

Somehow the two boats managed to get through the sampans without serious damage. Williams called on navy helicopters for assistance. The boatswain's mate had spotted some junks among the sampans and suspected that they were carrying ammunition.

Williams then decided to move his boats further down the canal and await helicopter gunship reinforcement. The PBRs turned a bend in the canal, some 150 yards away when, completely dumbfounded, they found themselves facing yet another concentration of junks, sampans, and troops even larger than that of the first engagement. Without hesitation, Williams put the 105 at full throttle, and both boats roared through the surprised enemy force and again scattered the craft, emerging on the far side without damage. By this time the helicopters had arrived, and Williams, with support from the air, once again led the two boats through the melee.

The entire battle lasted more than three hours, with Williams receiving a small piece of shrapnel in his side and his gunner taking a bullet through the wrist, which passed through so cleanly that no bones were broken. These were the only U.S. Navy casualties in this amazing action. The NVA forces lost well over 1,000 men and sixty-five vessels were destroyed. For his actions, Boatswain's Mate James Elliot Williams received the Medal of Honor.

The sailors of the Brown Water Navy are usually overlooked. Yet, during their service their duties were among the more hazardous performed by naval personnel. In 1968, for example, over 500 sailors attached to Operation Game Warden were awarded Purple Hearts for wounds. "One out of every three PBR sailors was wounded during his tour in Vietnam, many of those more than once." On the other hand, "one out of every five PBR sailors requested extensions of their tours, and many returned to Vietnam for repeat tours."[13] Thomas J. Cutler, a veteran of the Brown Water Navy, has penned the best epitaph for his shipmates: "They struggled with an inhospitable environment and faced a deadly enemy at point-blank range. Their courage is indisputable."[14]

NOTES

1. The UH–1 B and C could carry six men, the D and H models eleven. John Morrocco, *Thunder from Above: Air War, 1941–1968* (Boston: Boston Publishing Co., 1984), 70; John Morrocco, *Rain of Fire: Air War, 1969–1973* (Boston: Boston Publishing Co., 1985), 127; Edgar C. Doleman, Jr., and the editors of the Boston Publishing Company, *Tools of War* (Boston: Boston Publishing Co., 1984), 26, 69.

2. Unless otherwise noted, all material on the Bac Le Railroad strike, including the material on Olds, is from R. Frank Futrell, William H. Greenhalgh, Carl Grubb, et al., *Aces and Aerial Victories: The United States Air Force in Southeast Asia, 1965–1973* (Washington, D.C.: U.S. Government Printing Office, 1984), 58–60.

3. "Rumor had it that Puff could put one round in every square foot of a football field with just one pass." Edward F. Palm, "Tiger Papa Three: The Fire Next Time, Part Two," *Marine Corps Gazette* (February 1988): 70; Morrocco, *Rain of Fire*, 127. See also Larry Davis, *Gunships: A Pictorial History of Spooky* (Carrollton, Tex.: Squadron/Signal Publications, 1982).

4. Quoted in Jeffrey Ethell and Alfred Price, *One Day in a Long War:*

5. Thomas J. Cutler, *Brown Water, Black Berets: Coastal and Riverine Warfare in Vietnam* (Annapolis, Md.: Naval Institute Press, 1988), 43. See also Victor Croizat, *The Brown Water Navy: The River and Coastal War in Indo-China and Vietnam, 1948–1972* (Dorset, England: Blandford Press, 1984).

6. William C. Westmoreland, *A Soldier Reports* (Garden City, N.Y.: Doubleday, 1976), 217, 271.

7. The assault squadrons consisted of two divisions, one of thirteen ATCs (armored troop carriers), one CCB (command communication boat), and three monitors. The other division replaced a monitor with a refueler. Later, eight ASPBs (assault support patrol boats) were added to each division.

APCs were LCM conversions, known as "Tango boats," which were 56 feet in length, displaced 66 tons, had a draft of 3 1/2 feet, twin-screwed, and with a maximum speed of 8.5 knots. They were armed with one 20-mm cannon, two .50-caliber machine guns, two Mark 18 grenade launchers, and other small arms. The ATC had a crew of seven and could land a platoon of infantry. The well deck where troops rode was covered with a canvas awning for shade and to prevent grenades from being thrown among the troops. The ATCs were the only craft to retain the bow-ramp door, and was armed with plating and standoff armor to predetonate incoming rounds.

Monitors were also LCMs. They were used for heavy firepower and had a faired bow to increase speed. In addition to the weapons carried on the ATCs, the monitors had an 81-mm naval mortar amidships and a 40-mm cannon in a turret forward. Monitors were 60 feet in length, with a beam of 17 1/2 feet, had a displacement of 75 tons, and drew 3 1/2 feet of water. They carried a crew of eleven and had a speed of 8 knots.

The CCB was similar to the monitor, except that it had a command and control console amidships instead of the 81-mm mortar. The console contained HF, VHF, and UHF radios. The CCB also carried radar. The boats were flagships for the navy squadron and command posts for the army battalion commander.

The ASPB came into operation in late 1967. This 50-foot, 28-ton boat was specifically designed for the Mobile Riverine Force, and carried a crew of seven and had a strengthened hull designed to resist underwater concussion from mines. Its speed of 16 knots, weapons, which included an 81-mm mortar, 20-mm cannon, heavy machine guns, and grenade launchers, plus a chain-drag mine-countermeasures rig, made this boat the "minesweeper/destroyer for the force." Cutler, *Brown Water*, 240–246. See also Richards T. Miller, "Fighting Boats of the United States," *Naval Review* (1968): 297–329.

8. All quotes on the actions of Pfc. Davis are from Clark Dougan, Stephen Wise, and the editors of Boston Publishing Company, *The American Experience in Vietnam* (New York: W. W. Norton, 1988), 118–119.

9. Davis' wounds were nearly fatal, and he has had recurring health problems, including problems with Agent Orange. Dougan, *American Experience in Vietnam*, 119. See also Richard L. Schreadley, "The Naval War in Vietnam," *Naval Review* (1971): 180–209.

10. Unless otherwise noted, material on the U.S. Coast Guard in Vietnam is from Dennis L. Noble, "Cutters and Sampans," *U.S. Naval Institute Proceedings* 110 (June 1984): 46–53. Other material on the U.S. Coast Guard in Vietnam may be found in James A. Hodgman, "Market Time in the

Gulf of Thailand," *Naval Review* (1968): 36–67; and Eugene N. Tulich, *The United States Coast Guard in South East Asia During the Vietnam Conflict* (Washington, D.C.: U.S. Coast Guard, Public Affairs Division, 1975).

11. Cutler, *Brown Water*, 157.
12. All material on this engagement is found in ibid., 199–204.
13. Ibid., 206.
14. Ibid., 266.

Chapter 8

THE COUNTRY AND PEOPLE OF SOUTH VIETNAM

The combat artists not only captured war, but portrayed the country and people of South Vietnam. Like many of the American men and women who served in Vietnam, the artists perhaps did not understand the culture of Southeast Asia, but they did try to depict the countryside, urban areas, and people of South Vietnam. The diversity of the country is well represented by the works of Michael Bigbie, John Hart, and John

130. MICHAEL BIGBIE **Jungle Tree** 1974, Ink, 15½″ × 21¾″ (U.S. Army Center of Military Hist.)

T. Dyer, Jr. However, it is the people of Vietnam that I believe are best captured by the artists, especially the children. Read the passage by Kent Anderson on the children of South Vietnam and then closely examine the works by Trella Koczwara to see what war does to the innocents.

The former nation of South Vietnam contains a diversity of terrain and people. From the flat expanse of the Mekong Delta in the south, a narrow coastal strip of lowlands extends northeastward more than 500 miles along the South China Sea to the Demarcation Line along the 17th Parallel. Inland from this narrow strip of land, and beginning at about the 10th Parallel, the land rises abruptly into the Chaine Annamitique, which is dominated by jungles, with fertile plateaus in its southern portion. In 1965 the population of South Vietnam was put at 16.1 million, with the largest portion residing in the southern Delta region or along the narrow central coastal strip. Many American veterans have commented on the great beauty of South Vietnam and expressed a desire to return someday in peacetime to tour the country.

South Vietnam consists of three broad regions. The Delta is dominated by one of the twelve great rivers of the world,

131. JOHN HART
Marble Mountain 1967,
Watercolor (U.S. Marine Corps
Art Coll.)

136

the Mekong. Along with the Amur, the Yellow, and the Yangtze, the Mekong provides the drainage of the Asian continent into the Pacific Ocean. The 2,800-mile-long river is so heavily laden with silt that the delta formed where it meets the sea advances the coastline of the People's Republic of Vietnam some 250 feet per year.[1]

The southern region is low-lying and dominated by water. The soil is spongy, and the region was noted for the absence of a good road network. The nature of the area makes it an ideal location to grow rice, and more than 9,000 square miles were planted with this crop, causing the region to be known as the "rice bowl" of South Vietnam. The former capital of South Vietnam, Saigon, is located in this area.

The Central Lowlands extend along the South China Sea from the Mekong Delta northward to the Demarcation Line.[2] The region's width is anywhere from forty miles to a scant few miles. In general, the land is fertile, rice again being the main crop. The most fertile plains of the region stretch from Mui Dieu to Vang Da Nang. Fishing, of course, is also important in this area.

The Chaine Annamitique is a rugged 750-mile spur of the mountains in Tibet and China. The mountains are irregular

132. LARRY ZABEL
Rung Ho Sunset #3 [n.d.], Oil on aluminum, 24″ × 30″ (U.S. Navy Combat Art Coll.)

137

in height and have numerous spurs, which cut into portions of the Central Lowlands and almost reach the sea.

The northern portion of the mountains is narrow and very rugged; within the southern portion is a plateau area, known as the Central Highlands, that is about 100 miles wide and 200 miles in length. The peaks of the Chaine Annamitique range from a low of 5,000 feet to a high of 8,521 feet at Ngoc Ang.

The Central Highlands, an area of approximately 20,000 square miles, contain two distinct parts. The northern portion, called Cao Nguyen Dac Lac, stretches 175 miles north from the vicinity of Ban Me Thuot to the Ngoc Ang peak. This northern portion is very irregular, having elevations from 600 to 1,600 feet, with a few peaks much higher. The area covers some 5,400 square miles and is covered with bamboo and tropical forests and dotted with farms and rubber plantations. The southern portion of the Central Highlands contains some 4,000 square miles and has large areas over 3,000 feet in elevation. It is made up of tropical forests at the higher levels; bamboo grows at lower elevations. Coffee, tea, tobacco, and vegetables are grown in the fertile soil of the region.

Tim O'Brien describes how one soldier viewed the landscape in his area of the war: "The earth was red. He saw it first from the air, on the day he joined the war. A coral pink, brighter in some spots than in others, but always there. Later, . . . he saw it like film on the men's weapons and clothing and boots, under their fingernails, on their skins."[3]

The climate of South Vietnam, except in some mountain regions, is hot and characterized by a humidity that has been described as debilitating. The monthly mean temperature is 80° F, but it should be remembered that this is only an average reading, and days of over 100° are not unusual. Rainfall is "consistently heavy," with variations in temperature and rainfall amounts depending on the monsoons. In general, the winter monsoon, usually from October to April, brings a dry season, while the summer monsoon, beginning in June, brings the wet season. There are local variations in the monsoons. In the Mekong Delta, for example, the dry season lasts from December through March.

Most of the people who live in the lowland areas of South Vietnam are ethnically Vietnamese, with the exception of about 1 million Chinese, who live largely in the vicinity of Saigon. In 1965 the population contained some 400,000 Khmers (Cambodians) who lived in the Mekong Delta area. In the highlands, the most sparsely populated region in all of South Vietnam, the 1965 population estimates indicated some

700,000 people who are called by the Vietnamese the Nguoi Thuongs (highland people, frequently called Thuongs). In French, these people are called Montagnards (mountaineers), the term used most by foreigners to describe the mountain people. American troops shortened the French to simply "yards." Most ethnic Vietnamese look upon these people as backward.

Television news films and movies have made many Americans believe that most Vietnamese live in thatched huts. Indeed, with 75 percent of the population living in the country and after a brief examination of the housing of each region of the former South Vietnam, this is an easy stereotype to accept. In the Mekong Delta region, for example, the majority of the people live in villages with thatched roofs; in the Central Lowlands the predominant housing is much like that of the Delta, with fishing villages a little closer together. In the highlands, the Montagnards build their bamboo dwellings on pilings. Some tribes construct central longhouses; others construct tightly grouped houses along hillsides. Yet South Vietnam has cities teeming with life on crowded streets, and its former capital, Saigon, offered the sweet ambiance of Paris.

133. FRANK GERMAIN
Vietnamese Hamlet 1967,
Acrylic on illustration board,
42″ × 31″ (U.S. Air Force Art
Coll.)

134. ROBERT SCHAAR **Land of the Free** 1970, Acrylic, 27″ × 33″ (U.S. Air Force Art Coll.)

135. LEONARD H. DERMOTT **Imperial Palace** 1967, Pen with watercolor wash (U.S. Marine Corps Art Coll.)

136. ROGER BLUM
Catholic Church Near Gia Dinh 1966,
Ink, 9″ × 12″ (U.S. Army Center of Military
Hist.)

137. ALEXANDER A.
BOGDANOVICH **Buddhist
Shrine—Vietnam 1966**
1966, Acrylic, 25⅛″ × 25⅛″
(U.S. Army Center of Military
Hist.)

141

There are beautiful temples and churches. (The majority of the people are Buddhist, with a strong Catholic minority.) One reporter described the capital during the early stages of the war:

I found Saigon the most seductive of cities. . . . All the people I met, teachers, newspapermen, waiters and cabdrivers, were friendly and considerate. The women were beautiful, I thought, gliding along in their diaphanous costumes, and the spring weather was lovely, and the sidewalk cafes delightful. I walked along the tree-shaded avenues during the day and, lying in bed under the lazy ceiling fan in my room in the old Majestic hotel, listened to the sounds of the river traffic at night. As hordes of Western reporters were to in the years to come, I fell in love with Saigon.[4]

138. JAMES A. FAIRFAX **Buddhist Monk** 1969, Acrylic, 20″ × 30″ (U.S. Marine Corps Art Coll.)

142

139. TRELLA KOCZWARA   **Market Place Danang #1**   1971, Acrylic (U.S. Marine Corps Art Coll.)

140. JOHN T. DYER, JR.   **French School**   1966, Watercolor (U.S. Marine Corps Art Coll.)

141. JOHN T. DYER, JR.   **Continental Palace**   1966, Brown felt-tip pen on illustration board with watercolor wash, 22″ × 28″ (U.S. Marine Corps Art Coll.)

142. JOHN T. DYER, JR.   **Street Scene, Saigon**   1966, Pencil and brush (U.S. Marine Corps Art Coll.)

Nothing in their lives prepared young Americans for this Southeast Asian culture. Most of the soldiers, sailors, airmen, and marines were the products of television, technology, and the quick solution. Unable to comprehend a language based upon tones, most Americans tended to deride the Vietnamese language. The architecture seemed strange to their eyes, while the smells of Asia assaulted their olfactory senses. Yankees observed old men watching them intently with silent, unreadable faces. Beautiful women, in their graceful, flowing *ao dais*, seemed aloof. It is small wonder that most Americans could not adjust to this culture and quickly began to refer to their return to the United States as a return to "the world."

One of the tragic results of any war is the plight of innocent children. In the foreign wars of the twentieth century fought by American troops, there have been numerous instances of soldiers, sailors, airmen, and marines helping to establish homes and provide care for the children orphaned by war. Vietnam was no different. For example, marines helped to establish an orphanage at China Beach. Trella Koczwara has captured some of these children in her art.

Even the children of South Vietnam, exposed to the full fury of napalm, machine-gun fire, and high explosives, pointed out the differences between American and South Vietnamese culture. The small children seemed to some Americans to bear their trauma with a stoicism beyond their years.

143. THOMAS VAN SANT
Taxi 1968, Felt-tip pen, 10″ × 13″ (U.S. Marine Corps Art Coll.)

144. TRELLA KOCZWARA **Vietnamese Villager**   1970, Acrylic, 30″ × 30″ (U.S. Marine Corps Art Coll.)

146

145. JOHN STEEL **Portrait Study of Vietnamese** [n.d.], Acrylic (U.S. Navy Combat Art Coll.)

146. JOHN CHARLES ROACH **Portrait of a
Vietnamese Peasant** 1969, Pencil drawing,
12¼″ × 16″ (U.S. Navy Combat Art Coll.)

147. PETER GISH **Vietnamese Girl** 1967,
Oil, 33½″ × 46½″ (U.S. Marine Corps Art Coll.)

148

148. DOUGLAS ROSA **Children** 1967, Acrylic, 14″ × 18″ (U.S. Marine Corps Art Coll.)

149. RICHARD L. YACO **Innocence and Wire** 1968, Acrylic, 24″ × 32⅞″ (U.S. Marine Corps Art Coll.)

In Kent Anderson's novel, *Sympathy for the Devil*, the protagonist, Hanson, on an airliner in the United States, listens to a child crying:

> Hanson couldn't remember ever seeing any children cry in Vietnam, not even the ones who were wounded, who had flies crawling on their wounds and faces. He tried to think of at least one, but he couldn't.
>
> . . . [R]ecalling face after face, he met the same listless stare each time. Not that they seemed to blame him for whatever had happened to them, but they expected him to *do* something. Most of the time all he could do was wait for the medivac and watch them die.[5]

NOTES

150. TRELLA KOCZWARA **Seated Child** 1970, Felt-tip pen, 20″ × 24″ (U.S. Marine Corps Art Coll.)

1. All material on the geography and people of South Vietnam is found in Harvey H. Smith, Donald W. Bernier, Frederica M. Bunge, et al., *Area Handbook for South Vietnam* (Washington, D.C.: U.S. Government Printing Office, 1967), 1–22. For a detailed account of the history and people of

151. TRELLA KOCZWARA
Two Children 1970, Felt-tip
pen, 20″ × 24″ (U.S. Marine
Corps Art Coll.)

152. TRELLA KOCZWARA
**Vietnamese Girl and
Baby** 1970, Oil, 30″ × 36″
(U.S. Marine Corps Art Coll.)

151

Vietnam, see Frances Fitzgerald, *Fire in the Lake: The Vietnamese and the Americans in Vietnam* (Boston: Little, Brown, 1972).

2. The term "central" when speaking about the two broad geographical regions of South Vietnam means, strangely enough, "central only to pre-partition Vietnam and not to South Vietnam." Smith et al., *Area Handbook*, 10.

3. Tim O'Brien, *Going After Cacciato* (New York: Delacorte, 1978), 300–301.

4. Charles Kuralt, *A Life on the Road* (New York: G. P. Putnam's Sons, 1990), 71.

5. Kent Anderson, *Sympathy for the Devil* (Garden City, N.Y.: Doubleday, 1987), 58.

Chapter 9

WAR AND ART: ARTISTS AND THE U.S. MILITARY

The use of artists in the Vietnam War was not unique. Walls in Egyptian temples, Greek vases, Roman statues and arches, and works by Renaissance artists have depicted military scenes or the results of war. Brueghel's *Triumph of Death*, painted around 1562, shows the true face of war: death. Francisco Goya's passionate "response to war" did not "take a doctrinal stand, only a human one," according to Denis Thomas. Goya's heroes were usually the common people, and this is clearly shown in a series of eighty-two aquatints done between 1812 and 1823 under the title *The Disasters of War*. Until the invention of the camera in the nineteenth century, the work accomplished by artists was the only means the general public had of becoming visually aware of war.

The U.S. military has a long history of having artists record its activities, beginning with such men as John Turnbull, who sketched many military scenes during the American Revolution. One of his more noted military works is Cornwallis' surrender at Yorktown. Thomas Burch's depictions of naval victories are the best-known art produced during the War of 1812, the new nation's next major conflict. In both the Revolutionary War and the War of 1812, however, there is no record of artists actually basing their works on personal observations. With one exception, the military works produced prior to the Civil War were based on secondhand descriptions. The exception was the work of James Walker during the Mexican War (1846–48). Walker served as an interpreter for the army and, as an eyewitness, turned out twelve oil sketches. His large mural depicting the Battle of Chapultepec, however, was painted after the war.

The American Civil War (1861–65) marks the beginning of the use of eyewitness artists on a large scale in combat. The three broad classes of combat artists that emerged can still be used to describe those who attempt to record war through art. The first group of Civil War artists were amateurs. Most remained anonymous and generally undertook their work as momentos of their experiences. The second group were professionally trained and may or may not have actually witnessed the events. The last were professionals employed by the illustrated magazines. Cameras were then in use, but they were too bulky and could not capture movement. In other words, the photographer had to have subjects that were willing to remain immobile, thus preventing the capturing of actual combat scenes.[2]

Primarily responsible for the widespread use of artists was the rise of popular illustrated magazines such as *Century* and *Harper's Weekly*. The war artists attempted to provide the coverage of a pictorial magazine, similar to what *Life* achieved with photographs during World War II. That is, the artists sought to illustrate battles, along with scenes from behind the front, in order to provide a visual picture of the war's progress for the homefront. In general, the artists were successful, and some were highly prolific. Thomas R. Davis of *Harper's*, for example, is credited with 250 illustrations and covered more battles than any other artist.[3]

Winslow Homer was another artist who depicted the war. Homer, of course, went on to become more famous for the works he produced after the Civil War, especially his scenes of rural New England and seascapes. The works he produced during the war, such as *Prisoners from the Front* and *The War for the Union, 1862—A Cavalry Charge*, are still mentioned by critics. His pencil drawings, *Sketches of Soldiers*, provide an excellent look at the soldiers of the Union Army and, further, show a "remarkable feeling of movement."[4] Gordon Hendricks notes, however, that while Homer actually accompanied Gen. George B. McClellan for a short period of time during the push to reach Richmond in 1862, the "remainder of Homer's first hand Civil War contacts are in dispute." According to Hendricks, the artist produced most of his better works in his New York City studio. In fact, Homer's "work does not suggest immediate involvement in battle."[5]

The Civil War combat artists, as mentioned, also produced works that showed activities behind the lines. Some of these illustrations provide us with an understanding of everyday life in the nineteenth-century army. For example, James Walker's pencil drawing, *Row in Camp*, depicting soldiers brawling, gives graphic evidence that the men did not simply sit around campfires singing in a comradely fashion, as some popular myths may lead us to believe.[6]

The U.S. Army's long campaigns against the Native Americans west of the Mississippi River are documented by the noted artist Frederic Remington. Remington can be classed as a combat artist, for he actually accompanied troops in the field in actions against the Apache in the Southwest and the Sioux on the Great Plains. Over a century later, his art gives us some of the best surviving illustrations of the hardships of campaigning in the desert Southwest and the vastness of the Plains. Remington's studies of individual soldiers also provide us with a wonderful glimpse of the cavalryman and infantryman who made up the post–Civil War U.S. Army. It can be successfully argued that some of the artist's works do picture the army in a romantic and idealistic light. Indeed, the artist himself is reported to have remarked, "I paint for boys, boys from ten to seventy."[7] Remington, however, also produced works that belie the charge of putting the army in too romantic a light. For example, Remington is one of the few combat artists who portrayed the "enemy" in a sympathetic manner. At times it is difficult to tell who the artist felt more strongly about, the soldier or the Native American. Remington also accompanied the army in the Spanish-American War (1898). His *Charge up San Juan Hill* is probably the most recognized work to come out of that "Splendid Little War."

Edgar M. Howell notes that World War I "was a turning point in regard to 'war art,' " as governments now underwrote the use of art. The British and French used artists to help further their cause. Sir John Rothenstein noted that artists responded with "depths of emotion and technical powers which they had not hitherto been conscious of possessing . . . which they now possess no longer."[8] In 1917 the U.S. War Department decided to follow their allies' lead.

The army decided to commission a group of artists in the Pictorial Publicity Division of the Committee of Public Relations. Chosen to select a group of eight volunteers to be the official artists of the American Expeditionary Force (AEF) was one of America's leading illustrators, Charles Dana Gibson. Not surprisingly, six of the men Gibson selected were artist-illustrators: Harvey Dunn, Harry Townsend, George Harding, Walter J. Duncan, William Alward, and Wallace Morgan. J. André Smith was an architect who also etched. One "pure artist," Ernest Perxotto, was included in the group. The men were commissioned captains in the engineers. They were given no military training and, generally, were in France within two to three weeks after receiving their commissions. The artists were to supply sketches and paintings both for historical purposes and for use in periodicals and propaganda. A War Department memorandum of June 17, 1918, outlined a "general scheme" to utilize the new combat artists. The officers were to concentrate their efforts on troops in the trenches, in the training areas and in reserve, and on the lines of communication. The memorandum went on to state that an "elastic" work schedule was in force so that the artist could be used at locations which presented the "greatest opportunities." In nine months the eight men produced approximately 700 pictures of varying quality.[9]

The program, however, did not have an auspicious start. In the summer of 1918, for example, Major Kendal Banning, of the Historical Branch of the General Staff, wrote to artist-Captain Smith complaining that the official AEF artists' work to date lacked "action" and "human interest" and that "the officers of the General Staff" expressed very little interest in the works. Banning exhorted the AEF artists' contingent to produce works like those done by the French. In response to Banning's letter, Capt. William E. Moore, of the Photograph Sub-Section of the AEF, noted that he had "several other letters" of complaint about the program. Captain Moore agreed with some of the criticisms, but noted that after the artists had settled into their new routine, their products became superior to the early efforts. Other correspondence concerning Banning's letter indicated that all of the artists' superior officers were satisfied with the works. Major A. L. James, Chief of G–2–D, AEF, for instance, noted that the men were "doing extremely valuable work" in providing works for the historical record. Further, he felt that Banning was under the delusion that the artists were to be used to provide "action" scenes more suitable for recruiting and liberty-bond-drive posters. Eventually, the officer-artists were issued orders to concentrate their efforts on the advanced areas. To better understand the army's program, the role of Harvey Dunn is outlined.[10]

Dunn entered the army on March 7, 1918. Born March 8, 1884, to Tom and Bersha Dunn, on a prairie homestead in South Dakota, he became interested in art and studied under Howard Pyle, a noted illustrator. By the time the United States entered World War I, Dunn had established himself as an illustrator of note. He received commissions from *Harper's*, *Collier's*, *Century*, *Outing*, and *Scribner's*. The popular *Saturday Evening Post* used over 250 of his works.

Captain Dunn went to France with the goal of depicting the war as honestly as possible, showing "the shock and loss and bitterness and blood of it."[11] Dunn carried a portable scroll sketch box. The captain would do a sketch and then turn a knob to produce a clean working space for his next study. He traveled to wherever American soldiers were billeted: the Argonne Forest, the St. Mihiel Salient, and along the Marne River. According to his biographer, he went "over the top with the infantry, and . . . even commandeered an observation balloon to give ranges to an artillery battery."[12] One of his fellow soldier-artists complained that Dunn "would take the whole war home with him" in order to better produce his works. Dunn would make his rough sketches in the field and then do his finishing work later in a studio in Paris.

Dunn expected to spend several years at the War College finishing his artistic record of the Great War. He returned to the United States on February 9, 1919, and was "keenly disappointed" to learn that he was to be discharged on April 26. Years later, one of his students was to note that not being able to carry out his goal was the biggest heartbreak of the illustrator's life.

Some of Dunn's works for the army have great power and capture the horror, tiredness, and emotion of the American doughboy in the Great War. *The Harvest Moon* and *Out of the Wire* graphically illustrate death caused by modern war. *The Machine Gunner*, showing a stalwart doughboy ready for action, is probably one of the best-known pieces to come out of the war and has been used numerous times to illustrate books and articles on the AEF. There is no doubt that *The Boche Looter* and *Kamerad*, however, helped in the propaganda efforts against the Germans on the American homefront. Howell believes *Prisoners and Wounded* to be one of Dunn's best works. The pastel shows German prisoners carrying a stretcher while American wounded walk nearby and is "Dunn's most barren, most brutal way of saying that the hell of war is the shattered body and the wounded mind. Who [in this painting]," asks Howell, "is to be pitied, the prisoners, the wounded, or the guards? No matter which figure you look at, the victor is neither good nor evil, but the devil himself."[13]

The war greatly affected Dunn. According to Robert F. Karolevitz, the war made Dunn look with "far less enthusiasm . . . [upon] magazine and advertising illustration." Instead, he began to think about his early years in South Dakota and sought to paint some "significant and lasting pictures."[14] In pursuit of this goal, Dunn produced paintings of pioneer life on the windswept prairies, which have become his greatest legacy. Harvey Dunn died on October 20, 1952, at his home and studio in Tenafly, New Jersey.

The army, of course, was not the only service to have artists in uniform during the Great War. Capt. John W. Thomason, Jr., U.S. Marine Corps, produced many sketches of Leathernecks on the Western Front. Some of his drawings were also used to illustrate the short stories written by this talented but now largely forgotten officer.[15] Thomason, however, was a combat marine and did not serve as an artist.

Prior to the U.S. entry into World War II, Navy Lt. Cmdr. Griffith B. Coale organized navy artists into the Combat Artist Corps (CAC), and it is this group's title that led to the use of the official designation "combat artist" by the military. Coale himself produced the first piece of art for the new program, showing a navy escort of a convoy in the North Atlantic prior to Pearl Harbor.[16]

As early as February 1941, some museum officials recognized the value of using artists in the second global war. Eventually, every U.S. military organization in World War II, as well as the merchant marine, had men and women sketching and painting. As with the servicemen of the Civil War, the artists ranged from amateur to professional. This is not too surprising, for in a war fought mainly by civilian inductees, it is only natural that those with artistic talent would soon make themselves known. In 1943, for example, merchant seamen entered more than 150 works of art in a servicemen's art show in New York City. Hunter Wood, a chief boatswain's mate in the U.S. Coast Guard, witnessed the explosion and sinking of the British carrier *Avenger*. The event so moved Wood that he used the only artistic tools available to him at the time to record the death agony of the ship: ship's paint and canvas.[17]

The U.S. Marine Corps' art program was headed by Raymond Henri. The art works were produced by both civilian and military artists.

In 1942 the army, with the strong support of Secretary of War Henry Stimson, formed an Art Advisory Committee, under George Biddle, that was to select and assign artists to the various theaters of operations. According to one soldier-artist in the program, as soon as the artists began to work, "glowing reports flowed back stateside."[18] There were forty-two artists in the program, nineteen civilians and twenty-three soldiers. Biddle's instructions to the unit, in part, stated:

Any subject is in order, if as artists you feel it is part of War; battle scenes and the front line; battle landscapes; the wounded, the dying and the dead; prisoners of war; field hospitals and base hospitals; wrecked habitations; . . . character sketches of our own troops, . . . the nobility, courage, cowardice, cruelty, boredom of war. . . . Try to omit nothing; duplicate to your heart's content. Express if you can—realistically or symbolically—the essence and spirit of War. You may be guided by Blake's mysticism, by Goya's cynicism and savagery, by Delacroix's romanticism, by Daumier's humanity and tenderness; or better still follow your own inevitable star.[19]

Forty-five years later, Edward Reep, one of the artists in the program, was to comment that the freedom given to the artists "got the art group in hot water with certain members of Congress." Reep recalled that at least two members of Congress, Senator Theodore Bilbo and Representative Joe Starnes, "referred to money spent for artists on the field of combat as 'boondoggling.' "[20] This attitude stopped the program. Generals George C. Marshall and Dwight D. Eisenhower, however, partially reinstated the program, but only for soldier-artists.

David Longwell, executive director of *Life* Magazine, offered the army an option: *Life* would pay the salaries of the civilian artists and donate all completed works to the army. The army, in turn, would be responsible for transporting and housing the artists. This arrangement proved satisfactory to the army, and by war's end it had over 2,000 pieces of art in its collection. One student of military art notes that it was *Life*'s use of artists that made the periodical come closest to the "old tradition" of using special artists, as in the Civil War. Abbott Laboratories made a similar offer. The artists under this program provided the service with a number of scenes of medical activities during the war.[21]

The work produced by the many combat artists of World War II varies, with much falling in the range of very good to brilliant. One artist, Kerr Eby, is worth discussing here.

Eby was born in China in 1899, the son of a Methodist minister, and saw service as a sergeant in the engineers in World War I. The off-duty sketches he made in France were published in 1939 by Yale University under the title *War*. In World War II he was under accreditation to Abbott Laboratories and worked in the Pacific from 1943 to 1944. He died in 1946. Eby's works, according to one writer, leave the viewer with a feeling of men "fatigued to the very bone, . . . one-man units of a fatiguing horror so powerful, so all-engulfing," that they speak volumes on the effects of war.[22]

Eby's best works deal with his witnessing the 1943 invasion of Tarawa atoll by the U.S. Marine Corps. Betio, the island in the atoll attacked by the marines, measures only 800 yards at the widest and is 2 1/2 miles long. It took three days of intense fighting and cost the marines 1,000 dead, with 2,000 wounded, to secure the island. At one point, the invading marines had to wade over 700 yards through the water, under direct fire, just to reach the beach.[23] Eby's *Grapes of Wrath* shows an amphibious tractor that has received a direct hit with its crew sprawled in death. "I make no apology for drawings such as this," Eby is quoted as saying. "The official designation of my job was activities of the Marines and dying terribly . . . is one of those activities." In *Ebb Tide—Tarawa*, the bodies and body parts of dead marines are shown on the wires at ebb tide. The attack was made at flood tide, and when the sea rolled back it exposed the remains of the marines who had been cut down while trying to reach the beach. Eby's comment on this stark work: "In two wars, this I think is the most frightful thing I have seen."[24]

The ending of World War II brought difficulties for some of the military's art programs. The U.S. Marine Corps, for example, found that it lacked funding to provide proper storage for its art and was forced to disperse the works, mainly to the artists themselves. The Combat Art Corps of the navy was disbanded in 1960.

Some writers have very aptly labeled the Korean War (1950–53) the "Forgotten War." Complementing this title, the combat art of the Korean "police action" is relatively unknown. Howard Brodie, John Groth, Avery Chenoweth, and others have produced a number of works on the conflict. During this period, the U.S. Air Force's combat art collection came into being. At least 800 pieces of art, mainly from World War II, were transferred from the army to form the core of the air force's collection.

Thus, by the time of the Vietnam War, the U.S. military could claim a long tradition of using artists to depict their operations. In Southeast Asia the armed forces used both military and civilian artists, with the U.S. Air Force, U.S. Navy, and U.S. Coast Guard relying entirely on civilians. To better understand the combat art activities of the Vietnam War, one large program as well as the smallest—the U.S. Coast Guard's—will be illustrated.

The soldier-artists for the army's program were selected by the Center of Military History, the office in charge of both the army's historical and art programs. The soldiers first had to obtain permission from their commanding officers to undertake a temporary assignment to the combat art program. One of the major requirements for entering the program was the ability to record military events and to do so with strong emotional impact. The artists were given free rein to depict their subjects in their own style. The civilian artists in the program operated much like their predecessors in World War II. That is, the army paid all of their expenses to and from Southeast Asia and provided housing. The artists were then required to hand in all completed works within one year.[25]

The army's combat art in 1966 is a good example of how the program functioned for that service. In that year, thirty-six military and ten civilian artists recorded the Vietnam War. The soldier-artists, on temporary duty, worked in five-man

teams. They spent at least sixty days within Vietnam, sketching and photographing what they wished to portray. The soldiers then returned to Hawaii to produce studio works of their
preliminary sketches. Upon completion, the works were
turned over to the Center of Military History and the men
returned to their regular duties. Normally, the assignment
lasted from 120 to 135 days. The civilian artists worked in
much the same manner, but generally finished their works in
their own studios. Today, the army owns approximately 4,000
pieces of art dealing with the Vietnam conflict.[26]

The U.S. Coast Guard, the smallest of the five armed
forces, is not looked upon as a military force by most Americans. The image of lifesaver comes more readily to mind.
Yet the organization has served in every war of the United
States. The official art program of this service consisted of two
artists, Noel Daggett and Apollo Dorian.

Daggett studied at the California School of Fine Arts.[27] After
serving in the merchant marine and the U.S. Army, he worked
as an illustrator for the army in Heidelberg, Germany. When
he left the army, he returned to the United States and enrolled
at the Arts Center School in Los Angeles. Daggett also studied
at the Art Institute in Chicago and the New School in New
York.

In 1969 Daggett was invited by the U.S. Coast Guard to
tour Southeast Asia to record his impressions of the service's
activities. Of the twenty-five works he produced, at least
twelve focus on the role of the Coast Guard's 82-foot patrol
boats during Operation Market Time, which tried to cut off
the supply of arms to the Viet Cong from the sea.

Some of the more interesting civilian artists who served in
Vietnam include John Groth, who was the dean of the combat
artists in Southeast Asia.[28] Groth's art career stretched over
fifty years. In 1933 he became the first art director of *Esquire*.
His combat art experience began in World War II. Ernest
Hemingway once wrote that if "John had made his drawings
from any closer up front, he would have had to have sat in
the Krauts' laps." Groth went on to cover the Korean War,
the French war in Indochina, and then, finally, the U.S. experience in Southeast Asia. In addition to combat art, he en-
joyed portraying sports. His work has illustrated editions of
Mark Twain, John Steinbeck, Hemingway, and others. John
Groth died John 27, 1988, at the age of eighty-eight.

That women artists produced works for the U.S. military
is not well known. Two women are especially noted for their
efforts in Vietnam: Trella Koczwara for the U.S. Marine Corps
and Maxine McCaffrey for the U.S. Air Force.

Chris Joy Koczwara was born in New Jersey. She began to

take private art lessons at age thirteen and continued until she enrolled in the Ridgewood, New Jersey, School of Art in 1961.[29] She was invited to attend the Ringling School of Art in Sarasota, Florida, and did additional work at Fairleigh Dickinson University and Paterson State College in New Jersey. Upon completion of her studies, Koczwara began to exhibit her works in New York City and to teach children's art classes in Ridgewood.

At a Washington Square show in New York, she won notice for her paintings of still life and wildlife as well as landscapes and portraits. George Grey, of the Navy Combat Art Program, became interested in her work, which led to a voluntary assignment to the Electric Boat Company in Groton, Connecticut, where submarines are built, and to the U.S. Navy Submarine Base at New London, Connecticut. This assignment produced three large oils of about 40″ X 60″ each.

Koczwara's next assignment was being the only navy artist to record the launching of the *Apollo 7* spacecraft at Cape Canaveral, Florida, on October 11, 1968. The painting, which depicted the ignition and moment of liftoff of the rocket, later became a cover illustration of the prestigious U.S. Naval Institute *Proceedings*. It was this work that led Koczwara to Vietnam.

John Warner, Under Secretary of the Navy, had come to New York to view and accept an exhibition of naval art at the Salmagundi Club, the oldest professional art club in the United States. Koczwara was the youngest artist in the show and the first woman to be elected to the club. At this time Koczwara signed her works "Chris" Koczwara. Warner admired the *Apollo* painting so much that he is reported to have remarked, "I have to meet this guy," and was surprised to learn that the painter was a woman. The Under Secretary selected the *Apollo* painting to hang in his office in the Pentagon. Shortly thereafter, Warner asked Koczwara if she would be interested in going to Vietnam as a combat artist, and she accepted.

In 1970 Koczwara arrived in South Vietnam as a U.S. Marine Corps combat artist. She was scheduled to remain in-country for two weeks and to operate out of the Combat Information Bureau (CIB) at Da Nang. Some twenty years after her assignment, Koczwara recalled that when she arrived in South Vietnam her goals were to "see as much as possible" and to "present what I saw in a way in which viewers would perhaps feel or be stimulated to understand what was happening—or at least to see." She felt that her fellow combat artists were trying to cover the war "from all perspectives" and, since she was not "weapons knowledgeable," her work should try to "add to . . . [the] coverage" of the artists who were with combat troops. As with other civilian artists under the military combat art program, she was given "total freedom of expression . . . [and] interpretation" of the subject matter.

Immediately upon her arrival, Koczwara was restricted to the confines of the CIB because there was concern that the Vietnamese holiday of Tet would bring on increased enemy activities. This fact, and the realization that two weeks was "not enough time," led her to request a meeting with the commanding officer of the CIB. At the conference, Koczwara pointed out that she had not been able to get out of the press compound, which prevented her from carrying out her "purpose and assignment" in Vietnam. The artist went on to state that she "needed cooperation" to carry out her work. Furthermore, to cover the war in the best possible manner, Koczwara requested an extension of her time in-country, and the request was granted. Koczwara remained for three months, at her own expense, "to cover what was happening."

During that time in Vietnam, Koczwara managed to sample a large slice of activities. She flew in helicopters and visited a training center where scout and sentry dogs were trained. She spent time with the elite marines of the 1st Reconnaissance Battalion before and after they returned from patrols. She was made an honorary member of one of the battalion's companies. A photograph of Koczwara and members of Echo Company makes an interesting contrast: the five-foot, two-inch artist is surrounded and almost lost among large, grinning marines in camouflaged utilities, bush hats, and faces darkened for patrol. Koczwara also visited the hospital ship *Repose* and spent time at a China Beach orphanage.

Not surprisingly, the reaction Koczwara received among the marines she visited was one of amazement and curiosity. In a later interview, she said, "I spent a lot of time explaining what I was doing." Other comments by the Leathernecks were not so well phrased: "Who sent a woman *here*? A broad in Nam!" Koczwara, however, recalled that despite the curiosity and questions, she received cooperation wherever she went. At the end of her stay, she flew to Okinawa for two days before returning to the United States, arriving in New Jersey near the end of March 1970. Upon her return, she changed the signature on her works to Trella Koczwara, after a grandmother she admired. Trella then began to paint her Vietnam works.

Koczwara relied on what she describes as her "photographic" memory to produce eleven paintings over a one-year period. She also recalled what she smelled and sensed. In addition, she made sketches and photographs "*only* for *mechanical* detail." This was necessary, because a combat artist must operate in the field with no facilities, no materials, and no space, and time is always "of the essence." Her works are large, ranging in size from 40″ × 60″ to 60″ × 70″. The canvases are all big because Koczwara feels the subjects are big. War and the life and death "struggle—love of mankind"— cannot be contained in a small painting. Most important, the war "was a larger than life experience—and should exceed the TV screen size." Furthermore, Trella wanted the "viewer to become involved—not to walk by the artwork—but to stop and become involved—to think about it." The paintings have received wide acclaim at a variety of exhibitions.

Trella Koczwara continues to paint for the U.S. military, travels widely, and is a professor of art at Tennessee Technological University, Cookeville, Tennessee.

Maxine McCaffrey's illustrations appeared in periodicals such as the *Saturday Evening Post, Esquire, Redbook*, and others. She joined the U.S. Air Force Art Program in 1961 and painted a number of portraits of U.S. Air Force generals, such as Gen. Curtis LeMay. She donated over sixty works to the U.S. Air Force Art Program. Her works have been displayed at the National Gallery of Art in Washington, D.C., the New York World's Fair, and the U.S. Air Force Academy.[30]

McCaffrey concentrated on an aspect of the Vietnam conflict that very few people thought about during the long years of the war: the prisoners of war (POWs) of the U.S. Air Force. McCaffrey felt that most pilots were "quite bitter" about the apparent lack of concern on the part of the American people over the fate of the POWs. She quoted one pilot as stating that "our people choose to ignore them and probably hope they will die and go away. I sure haven't seen any protest marches organized about the POWs abuse!" McCaffrey related that the pilots she visited in South Vietnam "made me promise that I would paint one painting and dedicate it 'to our comrades up North' as they say it."[31] Some of McCaffrey's other works also show this feeling about missing airmen, such as *One Thunderchief Not Returning Today*, which is reproduced in chapter 7 (Illus. 107). Maxine McCaffrey died on August 20, 1979, in Los Angeles, California.

Some of the artists who depicted the Vietnam War were in the same danger as the combat soldiers, although no artist was killed during the war. Some had unusual experiences. Groth once noted another hazard: even during "skirmishes," if a soldier saw Groth sketching he would ask for a picture, and soon a group of soldiers would be bunching up around the artist, asking to have their portraits done, thus putting both soldiers and artist in danger. John T. Dyer, Jr., a U.S. Marine Corps artist, recalls awaiting a pickup by a helicopter at a "hot" landing strip. The procedure in cases where there was a chance for the helicopter to be shot was to run out to the aircraft, timing one's arrival just as any cargo was discharged and leaping aboard before the door was closed, thus allowing the machine the minimum amount of time on the ground. Dyer began a long 500-yard run, arriving just at the right moment to leap aboard, only to be waved off by a crewman. Apparently, there was to be no pickup by this helicopter. As the machine lifted, Dyer was left standing, out of breath, in the middle of a runway, a very good target. Fortunately, there was no incoming fire, and he managed to make his way safely back to a trench.[32]

One of the strangest incidents happened to George Dergalis while working for the U.S. Army and accompanying a detachment of the 82nd Airborne Division. While stopping at a village, Dergalis wanted to go near a river. The two soldiers assigned to protect him refused to go, as they could not properly protect him at that spot. The soldiers gave the artist a .45-caliber automatic pistol and a few grenades and told him to "scramble" down to the location, take a few pictures, and get back fast. Dergalis promised to follow the suggestion, but once there found the area "too tranquil" to hurry.

He sat and started to draw the small village. Suddenly, he found himself facing a Viet Cong soldier. Dergalis felt that his only option was to brazen his way out of the situation by continuing to draw. Many things flashed through the artist's mind, but he continued to sketch, only to find that the VC approved of his work and indicated that he wanted his portrait done. The Viet Cong apparently was satisfied with the result, for he patted him on the back and indicated that Dergalis was to remain there while he slipped into a hut. Returning, the man gave the American artist a framed picture of a Buddha. Dergalis then finished his original sketch of the village, got up, and waved good-by to the VC. When he returned, Dergalis found that the U.S. soldiers had been watching the whole scene but did not dare to fire.[33]

The artists accompanying the troops in the field were of necessity forced to carry a "mini" studio. Charles Waterhouse, a veteran of World War II and an artist for both the U.S. Navy and Marine Corps, recalled that in the field he carried a map case containing several sketchbooks, a paint set, and an Instamatic camera, and his pockets were stuffed with film and plastic bags to keep his work dry. The closest thing to a weapon that he carried was a knife.[34]

Even though the combat art of Vietnam offers contemporary Americans a visual method of understanding how people endured a war, the works of the Vietnam War have largely been overlooked. Why have the works of these men and women, some of whom have gone on to carve out excellent reputations in art circles, been overlooked? The simplest, and probably the best, explanation centers on a distrust of anything sponsored by the military or the government. Recalling the comment by James Jones quoted in the introduction about art sponsored by governments being propagandistic, one can understand that this feeling of distrust is of long standing. Add to this latent feeling the heat of the antiwar protests during the long course of the Vietnam War, and one can perhaps understand how this art form has been overlooked, or worse, not trusted. This feeling of distrust remains. One recent author has referred to the combat artists as "a few hired 'war artists' who dutifully illustrated patriotic clichés."[35] I believe that the reader will find most of the works contained within this book to be a far cry from patriotic clichés.

Art can be an extremely useful tool in understanding the face of war. The best of the combat artists, because they felt so strongly and with such great emotion about their subject, have been changed by their experiences. Harvey Dunn and Kerr Eby both were scarred by their experiences in war. Yet, it is this emotional catharsis that makes these works so valuable for those who wish to understand war. Without the deep emotions of the artist, perhaps the products would be nothing but propaganda, but with the emotion can come understanding for those who wish to see. Edward Reep, a combat artist from World War II, best states the reasons artists should be used to depict war:

The artist bequeaths a document of the uselessness, the anguish, and the savagery of war in the hope that future generations may avoid the pitfalls. Not even a camera records what the artist is able to perceive, for it is mechanical and bloodless and cannot detect right from wrong.

The war artist reveals that all wars are similar; the war artist's work relentlessly drums that message home. Through centuries of conflict, one constant persists, standing alone and above all others. Human lives are shortened, families are left homeless, children are orphaned, women and men widowed, and young warriors go all too early to their graves so that old men can win their senseless arguments.[36]

NOTES

NOTES

NOTES

NOTES

NOTES

NOTES

NOTES

NOTES

NOTES

1. Denis Thomas, *Arms and the Artist* (Oxford: Phardon Press, 1977), 3.

2. *Art of the Civil and Spanish American Wars, October 2 to November 10, 1980* (New York: Kennedy Gallery, 1980).

3. Pat Hodgson, *The War Illustrators* (New York: Macmillan, 1977), 16–17; Joseph F. Anzenberger, Jr., ed., *Combat Art of the Vietnam War* (Jefferson, N.C.: McFarland and Co., 1986), 6.

4. Gordon Hendricks, *The Life and Works of Winslow Homer* (New York: Harry N. Abrams, 1979), 66.

5. Ibid., 50.

6. *Art of the Civil and Spanish American Wars.*

7. Hodgson, *War Illustrators*, 28.

8. Edgar M. Howell, "An Artist Goes to War: Harvey Dunn and the A.E.F. War Art Program," *Smithsonian Journal of History* 2, no. 4 (Winter 1967–1968): 46.

9. Ibid., 46–47.

10. All material on the correspondence from Banning as well as the responses to his complaints is found in Correspondence Relating to War Artists of the AEF, Box 8, A.E.F., GHQ, G–2D, Record Group 120, National Archives Building, Washington, D.C.

11. Robert F. Karolevitz, *The Prairie Is My Garden* (Aberdeen, S.D.: North Plains Press, 1969), 36.

12. Ibid., 38.

13. Howell, "Artist Goes to War," 53.

14. Karolevitz, *Prairie Is My Garden*, 43. For further information on Dunn's prairie paintings, see Mari Sandoz, "The Look of the Last Frontier," *American Heritage* 12, no. 4 (June 1961): 41–53.

15. The only book-length biography of Thomason is Roger Willock, *Lone Star Marine: A Biography of the Late John W. Thomason, Jr., USMC* (Princeton, N.J.: Privately printed, 1961).

16. Anzenberger, *Combat Art*, 7; "Navy Art: A Vision of History" (Washington, D.C.: U.S. Navy, n.d.), 2–3.

17. Aimee Crane, ed., *Art in the Armed Forces: Pictured by Men in Action* (New York: Hyperion Press, 1944), 187–188, 208. Other countries also used artists in war. See John Paul Weber, *The German War Artists* (Columbia, S.C.: Cerberus Book Co., 1979).

18. Edward Reep, *A Combat Artist in World War II* (Lexington: University Press of Kentucky, 1987), xiv.

19. Ibid., xv.

20. Ibid.

21. Anzenberger, *Combat Art*, 7; Peter Johnson, *Front Line Artists* (London: Cassell, 1978), 173.

22. James Jones, *WW II* (New York: Grossett and Dunlap, 1975), 118.

23. Ronald H. Spector, *Eagle Against the Sun: The American War with Japan* (New York: Vintage Books, 1985), 259, 263–266.

24. Jones, *WW II*, 118, 120. For more information on Eby's works, see Kerr Eby, *War* (New Haven: Yale University Press, 1936).

25. "United States Army Art" (Washington, D.C.: Chief of Military History and Center of Military History, n.d.), 1.

26. Ibid.; Conversation, Marlou Gjeines, Army Art Curator, and Dennis L. Noble, September 27, 1990.

27. All material on Daggett is from an undated, unpaged photocopy

entitled "Noel Daggett," in the files of the Community Relations Division, U.S. Coast Guard Headquarters, Washington, D.C.

28. All material on Groth is from W. C. Heinz, "Sketching John Groth," *50 Plus* 26, no. 11 (November 1986): 42–49.

29. All material on Koczwara is from Bill White, "Lady Combat Artist," *Leatherneck* 71, no. 6 (June 1987): 40–45; Completed questionnaire, Trella Koczwara to Dennis L. Noble, October 31, 1990.

30. "Obituaries," *Air Force Times*, August 20, 1979, 26.

31. Quoted in Anzenberger, *Combat Art*, 101, 103.

32. Anzenberger, *Combat Art*, 26, 112.

33. Ibid., 17, 20, 23.

34. Charles Waterhouse, *Vietnam Sketchbook: Drawings from Delta to DMZ* (Rutland, Vt.: Charles E. Tuttle, 1968), 7.

35. Lucy R. Lippard, *A Different Kind of War: Vietnam in Art* (Seattle: Real Comet Press, 1990), 10.

36. Reep, *Combat Artist*, 200.

THE LITERATURE AND FILMS OF THE VIETNAM WAR

William J. Palmer

> You know how it is, you want to look and you don't want to look. I can remember the strange feelings I had when I was a kid looking at war photographs in *Life*... even when the picture was sharp and cleanly defined, something wasn't clear at all, something was repressed that monitored the images and withheld their essential information.
> —Michael Herr, *Dispatches* (1977)

When American involvement in the Vietnam War ended, first in 1973 with the withdrawal of American troops and then again in 1975 when South Vietnam finally fell, the nation's attitudes toward that long and disappointing conflict were confusingly fragmented. Vietnam veterans, who had served "in-country" Vietnam, who had witnessed the deaths of comrades and had experienced firsthand the confusion of war, had returned to a "world" unwilling to recognize their efforts, at times unwilling even to acknowledge their existence, or, at other times, more than willing to condemn them for their participation. These veterans could not get the war out of their minds.

Most Americans, however, wanted to put the war out of their minds, forget it, write it off as a bad debt, pretend it never happened. In fact, for about four years after the humiliating withdrawal from Vietnam in 1973, and two years after the tragicomic fall of Saigon in 1975 (complete with helicopters being bulldozed off the decks of aircraft carriers), most Americans did not even want to think about the Vietnam War. The soldiers who fought there certainly did not want to talk about it, and the New York publishing industry and the Hollywood film industry, perhaps rightly so, figured that nobody wanted to spend money to read about it or watch it re-created on movie screens. The result was that American culture was provided by the literary and media establishments with a nice little four-year decompression chamber.

Actually, this void of literary and film representations of the war from 1973 to 1977 was nothing new. During the ten years of American military involvement in Vietnam, only one major American motion picture, *The Green Berets* (1968), produced by John Wayne's Batjac production company, even attempted to deal with the war in realistic, contemporary terms. Unfortunately, it was not an honest attempt. *The Green Berets* turned out to be a blatant rightest exercise in militarist propaganda presented in the familiar style of the John Wayne western. In *The Green Berets*, all the baggage of classic westerns like *She Wore a Yellow Ribbon* and *Fort Apache* was simply packed up and transported directly from the Monument Valley to Southeast Asia. Fort Apache became a beleaguered firebase in Vietnam; the Indians became the Viet Cong, and the Air Cavalry came thumping to the rescue in choppers. Other films, such as *The Wild Bunch* (1969) and *M*A*S*H* (1970), commented metaphorically on the Vietnam War during the period the war was going on even though their stories were set in different times and different locales. Only *The Green Berets* actually tried to represent the war. But it badly bungled the job.

There were more literary representations of the Vietnam War while the war was in session than there were films, but not many. The best of these works of fiction and nonfiction were more successful at offering realistic portrayals of the war than had been *The Green Berets*. Along with William Eastlake's *The Bamboo Bed* (1969) and David Halberstam's *One Very Hot Day* (1967), Daniel Ford's novel *Incident at Muc Wa* (1967), written and published while the war was still going on, and eleven years later made into the film *Go Tell the Spartans* (1978), was one of the first realistic novels about the Vietnam War. It was a startlingly prophetic novel, though not nearly as prophetic as Graham Green's *The Quiet American* (1956). The plot of Ford's novel embodies the thoughtless futility of the American presence in Vietnam. It involves an old French outpost that the Americans do not want to garrison and the Viet Cong have no desire to attack, which nevertheless becomes the site of a major firefight. The book was written a year before the famous siege of Khe Sanh was "won" and the encampment abandoned.

In the years 1962–1973, when American troops were actively involved in the Vietnam War, films like *The Green Berets* and novels like *Incident at Muc Wa*, which attempted to deal with the most important ongoing event in contemporary American history, were the exception rather than the rule. From 1973 to 1977, the American literary and film media threw a curtain of silence over the portrayal of that event. Simply put, perhaps out of fear, perhaps out of guilt, perhaps out of embarrassment, no one wanted to deal with Vietnam. All that suddenly changed in 1977.

That year, two nonfiction memoirs, *A Rumor of War* (1977) by Philip Caputo and *Dispatches* (1977) by Michael Herr, appeared. These two works were the point men for a highly impressive body of literature generated out of the Vietnam War that would surface in the next fifteen years. That body of Vietnam War literature is always about humanity at its furthest outpost. Every one of the major works on this war pays homage to Joseph Conrad's view of man's potential heart of darkness. Vietnam War literature is also like science fiction. It deals with Americans launched into a whole new galaxy where everything is different and beyond their understanding, where they have to learn to survive. The best Vietnam literature is always about the grunts, "the unwilling working for the unqualified to do the unnecessary for the ungrateful." In Vietnam there were seven support personnel for every grunt. But always the grunts found themselves out there alone, driven back on themselves as their only means of survival.

Finally, Vietnam War literature is about illusion and confusion. Life in the war becomes life in a world where nothing is ever what it seems to be, where the rules keep changing, where everything is a swirling mystery and no such thing as graspable reality exists, where understanding is out of the question, way too much to ask, and survival is all that one can ask. A massive body of Vietnam War literature, both nonfiction and fiction, has accumulated since 1977, but a few books have already claimed their place as the classics of this subgenre.

Caputo's *A Rumor of War* won the Pulitzer Prize in 1977. It is a conventional but tellingly written story of his own "John Wayne wetdream" of becoming a Marine, fighting in a war, and losing all of his romantic illusions. Caputo was a member of the first designated American combat unit assigned to Vietnam. He landed at Da Nang in 1964 with a cocky crew who, to use his words, couldn't wait to fight that "splendid little war." But Caputo quickly realized that he did not understand what was going on in Vietnam and that his macho romanticism was as false as the whole facade of Marine Corps bravado that had been drilled into him in boot camp. He cracked under those realizations. This book is a tortuously honest self-examination of how the civilized side of human nature can break down in a war. In the end, Caputo becomes involved in an atrocity and is brought up on court-martial charges for the murder of two Vietnamese civilians.

Michael Herr's *Dispatches* did not win the Pulitzer in 1977, but it did set the artistic standard for all of the Vietnam War literature, both fiction and nonfiction, to follow. Written in an autogetum "rock and roll" style, and telling the grunts' stories as if they were telling them themselves, Herr captured the mythic despair and the black romanticism of Vietnam better than any other writer before or since. In the twenty-first century, when someone wants to know about the Vietnam War, *Dispatches* will be the surviving nonfiction classic to which they will turn. As Ernie Pyle did in World War II, Michael Herr writes about the grunts. *Dispatches* is a graphic, personal piece of journalism that gives you the feel of the war by means of what Herr calls "illumination rounds" (short bursts of stunning symbolic episode, anecdote, dialogue, or description). To do this, he invented his rock and roll style, a frenetic, amplified, white-hot, dope dream style à la Jimi Hendrix and Jim Morrison. Listen:

"Quakin' and shakin'," they called it, great balls of fire. Contact. Then it was and the ground: Kiss it, eat it, fuck it, plow it with your whole body, get as close to it as you can without being in it yet or of it, guess who's flying around your head and your body too, the space you'd seen a second ago between subject and object wasn't there anymore, it banged shut in a fast wash of adrenaline. Amazing . . . the reserves of adrenaline you could make available to yourself, pumping it up and putting out until you were lost floating in it, not in it, actually relaxed. Unless of course you'd shit your pants or were screaming or praying or giving anything at all to the hundred-channel panic that blew word salad all around you and sometimes clean through you. Maybe you couldn't love the war and hate it inside the same instant, but sometimes those feelings alternated so rapidly that they spun together in a strobic wheel rolling all the way up until you were literally High On War, like it said on all the helmet covers. Coming off a jag like that could really make a mess of you.[1]

If Michael Herr's *Dispatches* is the stylistic benchmark of the literature of the Vietnam War, Tim O'Brien's *Going After Cacciato* (1978) is the finest work of fiction that has been written about the Vietnam War. It is also different from all the other major Vietnam books, both fiction and nonfiction. Most Vietnam War books recreate the physicality, the "feel" of the war, the way things happened. Yet there is a sameness of perception about all of them. They are mired in conventional realism. They represent war stories. *Going After Cacciato* presents all of the physical events of the war, but it is also very aware that reality can constantly shift its shape, can be symbolic as well as merely physical, can be projected into the future as well as merely remembered. The war in *Going After Cacciato* is a war of strictly personal survival taking place inside the mind, fought by the human imagination.

Going After Cacciato is a violent book in which deaths occur, the heart of darkness is glimpsed, enigmatic uncertainty prevails. But it is also a quiet, gentle book that affirms the potential for simple human good in a world terminally metastasized with mega-evil. It all begins when a soldier named Cacciato decides to walk away from the war, packs up and starts west for Paris, good old Gay Paree, some 8,600 miles away. The third squad goes after him, ordered to bring him back. After all, you can't have deserters in a war. They actually get him in sight, start moving up the small grassy hill where he is camped—then everything gets complicated. Reality starts to shimmer and glint.

The novel focuses upon the mind of Paul Berlin, one of the soldiers of the squad going after Cacciato. The narrative interiorizes, and time splits into a number of distinct dimensions. The plot of *Going After Cacciato* is presented in terms of this complex time structure. Present time begins the novel as the squad takes off after Cacciato. Future time, into which we are periodically flashed forward, consists of ten short chapters spread throughout the narrative, all titled "The Observation Post." In these chapters, Paul Berlin stands guard all night in a tower overlooking the South China Sea and thinks about the war. Past time takes two forms: flashbacks of Paul Berlin's recent past made up of all the events of his six months in Vietnam; and flashbacks of Paul Berlin's distant past, his growing up in Wisconsin. Finally, the fifth and most important time zone is one we might call "imaginative time." It consisted of Paul Berlin's fantasy of the possibility of the squad actually following Cacciato all 8,600 miles to Gay Paree, where the peace talks are being held.

All of these time zones are necessary forms of reality within which the combat grunt lives, by which the combat grunt survives, in and out of which the combat grunt constantly moves. The war is always the same, and the goal of the men is always the same: "The only goal was to live long enough to establish goals worth living for still longer" (43). Above all else, the only goal of the combat grunt was survival—survival pure and simple and unadorned. The glory of this book is Paul Berlin's constant struggle to escape and survive the physical events of the war. To do this, he uses the only tool he has available, his imagination. This novel is mainly about imagination, about the ability of human beings to write their own lives, to be novelists. It is a brilliant metafiction, a fiction about the imaginative creation of fictions—but it goes one step further. It affirms the possibility that the created fiction can actually become reality. In fact, it affirms the necessity of the created fiction becoming real. It is through this leap of faith that the war becomes bearable for Paul Berlin.

The journey after Cacciato to Paris, which is Paul Berlin's imaginative means of survival, takes the form of a Crosby and Hope road movie for the dope generation. The journey is a series of obstacles or ambushes of an almost "Perils of Pauline" sort. Again and again, the squad gets imprisoned or cornered, but Paul Berlin always comes to the rescue in the nick of time. How? He imagines them out of danger, imagines every minute detail of the escape. *He thinks, therefore it am.* His imagination holds the ultimate power of survival in the world of the journey, in the world of the war.

The Vietnam of the mind is all that exists now. It is a dangerous, surreal place where nothing is ever what it seems. It is all of our lives at one point or another. It is a place that we want to survive but that we know we can never escape. *Going After Cacciato* offers a way of dealing with this sort of world.

Going After Cacciato is not really a "war novel." It is a novel that celebrates the power of the human spirit we all share, celebrates our power in the worst of all possible human situations, celebrates our power to survive and triumph no matter how oppressive or imprisoning reality may become, celebrates our power of imagination in the face of reality as does any genuine work of art, be it novel or film or painting.

The 13th Valley (1982) by John Del Vecchio takes yet a different approach to the fictional representation of the Vietnam War. It is the most intellectual of all the Vietnam War novels, a volatile mix of philosophy, history, politics, emotion, and extremely graphic war reality. It tells the day-by-day, hour-by-hour, and mad-minute-by-mad-minute story of an operation that turns into a major firefight in the virgin Khe Ta Laou Valley north by northwest of Hue. It follows a single airmobile company, one of six participating in the sweep of the valley.

This heavy emphasis on the step-by-step unfolding of a major infantry operation in Vietnam is the answer to any history buff's prayers. When, where, and, in exact detail, how it was done is presented meticulously and accurately as well as dramatically. The author even supplies topographical maps and actual brigade-level "SIGNIFICANT ACTIVITIES" reports for each day of the sweep. Eventually, however, this historical approach becomes a source of tremendous irony. After reading about every treacherous step the "boonierats" of Alpha Company have taken, then reading the official, acronym-choked, impersonal "SIGNIFICANT ACTIVITIES" report, the reader realizes how little of reality official paperwork—the material on which historians rely—really conveys. This counterpoint between the official historical documents and the real human history being made is powerful and enlightening.

The main characters of *The 13th Valley* are Brooks, a black 1st lieutenant with a college degree in philosophy; Egan, the best soldier in the company, holder of an engineering degree, whose answer to everything is "It don't mean nothin' "; Cherry, a new man in his first week in-country; Jan, an angry, politicized black man around whom the novel's complex study of racism swirls; Silvers, nicknamed "The Jew," a writer; and El Paso, the Chicano radio operator, who has a college degree in history. As Brooks put it, "We all have different methods of ordering the world around us."

Alpha Company is one of the more highly educated collection of grunts going. The result is a running discussion in which the verbal combatants attempt to define and redefine the war and its causes, to fit the war into the theoretical parameters of their own particular discipline. There is a tremendous amount of reality in *The 13th Valley*, but there is an equal amount of historico-philosophical speculation. Not satisfied with being "merely" a novel, it tries simultaneously to be a military history, a cultural study of racism, a philosophical treatise on the nature of war. The miracle is that it manages to juggle all of these intentions so well.[2]

While the publication of *A Rumor of War* and *Dispatches* in 1977 triggered the formation of what by the 1990s has become a full and strong subgenre of Vietnam War literature, it was also about that same time that the American film industry decided that American mass culture was ready to refocus its attention on Vietnam.

In the late seventies, the Vietnam War films, specifically *Coming Home*, *The Deer Hunter*, *Go Tell the Spartans*, and *Apocalypse Now*, served as barometers that measured the submerged public opinion toward the war and the soldiers who fought in it. These movies indicated that beneath the surface of American society there was a thoughtful sympathy for and understanding of the situations of the veterans who fought and survived the war as well as a historical curiosity as to how the war was fought and what the war meant. That cluster of films changed America's whole attitude toward the Vietnam

War and the veterans who had fought it. If anyone ever needed evidence of the power of mass media to influence the cultural mind-set of a nation, the impact of those films would provide it. Though they did not always accurately portray Vietnam, its people, or the war fought there, they did catch the attention of American culture and convince the American people that it was finally time to reconsider the war in all its dimensions.

In the eighties, however, the social interest in the Vietnam War lost its immediacy with increased assimilation of Vietnam veterans into American society. Curiosity about the war had been satisfied by the outpouring in the late seventies of both the films and the many excellent books about the war. Yet, a number of particularly eighties events kept the Vietnam War alive, not as a social issue but as a meta-issue, a cautionary metaphor from the seventies for other eighties issues. The unique set of events that kept eighties' America attuned to the lessons of the Vietnam War included the Russian invasion of Afghanistan in late 1979, the failure of the hostage rescue mission into Iran, the increasing American presence in Central America, the loss of life and the withdrawal of troops from Beirut, and finally the Persian Gulf War of 1991. In all of these cases, the Vietnam War was repeatedly cited as a text for contemporary comparison, a precedent for American failure. Political voices used the Vietnam War to make points about the political choices open to the Reagan administration in Central America. Vietnam veterans used the war for political leverage and pushed a number of issues relevant to their reinstated voices. These issues kept alive American social consciousness of the legacy and the continuing quest for meaning of the Vietnam War.

In the late seventies and burgeoning throughout the eighties, simultaneous to all of this mass cultural attention (in movies, TV, and the print media), the academic establishment discovered the Vietnam War. English departments generally were the first to offer courses in the war, because by 1979 an impressive body of literature had been published. Political science and history departments also began creating Vietnam War courses. National literature conferences regularly scheduled sessions on the teaching and scholarship of the Vietnam War. By the late eighties, conferences dealing exclusively with the Vietnam War began to appear. The month of April 1988 is a good example of this increased fascination with the Vietnam War in the college classroom. Three full conferences— the American Studies Symposium at Purdue University, the Wisconsin Conference on the Teaching of History at the University of Wisconsin Centers, Waukesha, and a national Con-

ference on the Teaching of the Vietnam War sponsored by
the Indochina Institute of George Mason University in Washington, D.C.—were held that focused exclusively upon the Vietnam War.

The years 1977 to 1979 marked the real turning point in Vietnam War consciousness-raising stimulated mainly by mass culture. When the Vietnam War films of 1977–79 made money and won Academy Awards, it served notice that American society was ready to talk about Vietnam, that the healing had begun.

Vietnam remained a fascination in movies, in books, in classrooms, and in the American social consciousness all through the eighties because it had become a metaphor for what America was afraid it was going to become in the economic and political cold war with the Soviet Union and Japan: a loser. Vietnam became a warning, a symbol of defeat and loss, but most of all, it became a text.[3] It became an extremely complex text that was constantly being interpreted, reinterpreted, and exploited all through the eighties.

In the eighties, the Vietnam War continued to exist in the obsession of American film with it. Throughout the decade films of every genre employed Vietnam as text or subtext. For example, *Off Limits* (1988) is both a Vietnam War film and buddy-chase thriller like *Lethal Weapon* (1987) or *To Live and Die in L.A.* (1986). *Off Limits*, however, happens to be set in Saigon in 1968 rather than in San Francisco or L.A., which changes the whole context of violence in this film. "In a war," as Samuel Popkin has stated, "the first and foremost issue is the containment of violence."[4] Dirty Harry, operating in San Francisco, is trying to contain violence in that city. Harry has a gun and the bad guys have guns, but everybody else is unarmed. In *Off Limits*, literally everybody has a gun—good guys, bad guys, innocent bystanders, and children. The violence has escalated to the point where the buddy-cop genre movie is no more than a text within a bigger text, a small war caught in the context of a larger war, a microcosm of the Vietnam War's macroviolence. In the eighties, films like *Platoon* (1986), *Off Limits*, *Full Metal Jacket* (1987), or *Hamburger Hill* (1987) provided fuel for the American imagination because that is where the real text of the Vietnam War now resides.

A substantial body of Vietnam War films has accumulated into a rather full subgenre in the years since 1977. The history of the Vietnam War film is a clear one. Beginning in 1977, the Vietnam War film has progressed through three rather clearly delineated phases: (1) the Epic Phase, (2) the Comic

Book Phase, and (3) the Symbolic Nihilist Phase. Folded or layered into these three phases are the three major themes that dominate the Vietnam War films: (1) life in the war itself (adaptation, survival, loss of innocence, change, morality); (2) the meaning of the war; and (3) coming home from the war. Some themes are much more prominent in some phases of this timeline than in others.

By far the most explored of these three themes is the third, coming home. Thus the Vietnam War films are a text both of the war and of the postwar reentry of the soldier into "the world," as he called it. The first or Epic Phase (1977–79) was a traditional, story-oriented text, a war text aligned with the traditions of twentieth-century American literary and film war texts. In one sense, the films of the Epic Phase were all clichés. How different, for example, is the journey through the Vietnam War of Captain Willard (Martin Sheen) in *Apocalypse Now* from that of Henry Fleming in Stephen Crane's *The Red Badge of Courage*? How different, for example, are training camp to combat films like *The Boys in Company C* from the dozens of movies of the same type made about earlier wars, from *Sergeant York*, to *To Hell and Back* to *The Sands of Iwo Jima* to *Darby's Rangers* to *The Devil's Brigade* to *The Dirty Dozen* to *The Big Red One*? It is no coincidence that two of the earliest and most powerful books about the Vietnam War, Philip Caputo's *A Rumor of War* and Gustav Hasford's *The Short Timers*, choose a conventional structure to present their versions of the evolution of the Vietnam War Everyman soldier. Thus, the Epic Phase, with its story orientation, its generative linearity of character development, its traditional structures and themes, is the modernist phase of the Vietnam War film industry.

Phase Two, the Comic Book Phase, is a text corrupted mainly by Reagan administration chauvinistic rhetoric. In speeches throughout the eighties, President Reagan valorized the idea that America did not really lose the Vietnam War and that the war can be refought and rewon in places such as Grenada, Central and South America, and the Middle East. This valorization by an extremely popular president cleared the way to profitability for a whole series of "return to Vietnam and do it right this time" propagandist fantasies in the period 1980–86. John Rambo was the Sergeant Rock of this Reagan administration war comic. In 1986, as his comic book image, more often than not draped in the American flag, appeared on the covers of *Time* and *Newsweek* and in the pages of every newspaper and magazine in America, John Rambo, né Sylvester Stallone, was invited to the White House and treated as if he were a real Congressional Medal of Honor winner. Perhaps this Comic Book Phase of the Vietnam War films is one of the best examples of the manner in which American film and orchestrated (propagandist) social history can complement one another.

Only Phase Three, the Symbolic Nihilist Phase of 1987–88, makes an honest attempt to portray the Vietnam War in ways that film as medium best deals with human experience, history, and ideas. These films are a significant advance in the American perception of the Vietnam War. In general, they eschew story and, while focused on stereotypical characterization, attempt to capture the moments, the confusion, and the chaos of the war in the same way that the illumination rounds of Michael Herr's *Dispatches* did through his remarkable postmodernist style. These movies of Phase Three do not generally attempt to impose order on a primary text that had no order. In the case of *Platoon*, when such an attempt to impose the order of the story is made, that attempt pales in the face of the consistently deconstructing text. When these Phase Three movies succeed, they capture the existential feel of disorder, confusion, and utter meaninglessness that came to be this war's essential emplotment. Thus, the 1987–88 phase of Vietnam War film history is its postmodernist phase, a series of films that consciously deconstruct the war, which was consistently deconstructing itself even as it was going on. In these films, all the myths of the Vietnam War are consistently undermined.

The Epic Phase is comprised of four major films—*Coming Home*, *The Deer Hunter*, *Go Tell the Spartans*, and *Apocalypse Now*—and a number of minor films such as *Who'll Stop the Rain*, *Heroes*, *Rolling Thunder*, and *The Boys in Company C*. Only two of these movies, *Apocalypse Now* and *Go Tell the Spartans*, are actually fully set in Vietnam. The Epic Phase is so named based on the nature of its two most important films, *The Deer Hunter* and *Apocalypse Now*. Both are films of epic scope. *The Deer Hunter* reigned for twelve years as *the* epic treatment of the coming home theme, while its major competitor at the 1978 Academy Awards, *Coming Home*, was but a domestic, soap-opera treatment of that theme. In the final month of the eighties, however, *Born on the Fourth of July* proffered a challenge to *The Deer Hunter*. *Apocalypse Now* is still unsurpassed as *the* Vietnam War epic.

From 1980 to 1986 the Vietnam War entered its Comic Book Phase. The two Rambo sequels and the POW rescue movies such as *Uncommon Valor* and Chuck Norris' three *Missing in Action* shoot-em-ups are the best examples of the rampant exploitation of the war and Vietnam veterans in American society and media. This comic book approach involves the creation of shallow, stereotyped military or commando characters of the sort that appeared in comic books like *G.I. Joe*, *Men at War*, or *Sergeant Rock*. These stereotyped characters take the form of either a single, larger-than-life fighting machine like Sergeant Rock or a commando team of specialists (usually a demolition expert, an inventive tactician/con man, and a strongman as in the TV series *Mission Impossible* or *The A Team*) led by an officer/administrator. Ironically, *Apocalypse Now* was originally conceived, in its first script version by John Milius, as a sort of G.I. Joe comic book set in Vietnam.

In describing that first script of *Apocalypse Now*, Francis Ford Coppola said:

> The script, as I remember it, took a more comic-strip Vietnam War and moved it through a series of events that were also comic strip: a political comic strip. The events had points to them—I don't say comic strip to denigrate them. The film continued through comic strip episode and comic strip episode until it came to a comic strip resolution: Attila the Hun (i.e. Kurtz) with two bands of machine-gun bullets around him, taking the hero (Willard) by the hand, saying "Yes, yes, here! *I have the power in my loins*!" Willard converts to Kurtz's side; in the end, he's firing up at the helicopters that are coming to get him, crying out crazily. A movie comic strip. . . . That was the tone and the *resolution*. The first thing that happened after my involvement was the psychologization of Willard.[5]

Coppola's vision of the war was more expansive, psychological, and literary than was Milius' shallow, pop culture, comic book approach. But since that time Hollywood writers, producers, and directors have much more often opted for the comic book vision.

This comic book approach, however, fails in "contextualizing" history. Film needed to find a way to represent the Vietnam War as the complex political, social, and psychological event that it was. Nevertheless, in the brief history of the Vietnam War film, the bulk of the films have subscribed to the comic book approach. That bulk of films is flattened by the comic book simplifying of the issues of the Vietnam War and the choice of noncredible action over human characterization. In *Rambo II* (1986) and *III* (1988) there is no concern whatsoever for John Rambo as a person, a returned, grieving, and alienated Vietnam veteran as in *First Blood*. The only concern is for John Rambo as killing machine, similar to the high-tech Russian helicopter he confronts in *Rambo III*.

Not all of the comic book characters of this second phase are action figures out of Marvel Comics, however. Richard Pryor plays a Vietnam POW as a black Bugs Bunny in the coming home film *Some Kind of Hero* (1981), and the sequel to *American Graffiti* (1973), *More American Graffiti* (1979), portrays the Vietnam generation as if they were characters in Archie comic books. *The Stunt Man* (1980), however, is one film from this period worth noting. It is possibly the most artful and sophisticated of all the veteran-coming-home Vietnam films. In *The Stunt Man*, life and the Vietnam War are metaphorically represented as movie. An anonymous Vietnam veteran joins the crew of a movie company making a World War I movie; suddenly, his sense of never knowing what is going on, of what is real and what is just an illusion, comes flooding back to him as a strange sort of variation on a Vietnam War flashback. *The Stunt Man* is the only comic movie of the Comic Book Phase actually to strive for any symbolic or characterizational depth.

In portraying the issues of the Vietnam War as movie, *The Stunt Man* shares its central metaphor with Julian Smith, who wrote:

Vietnam was like a movie that had gotten out of hand: gigantic cost overruns, a shooting schedule run amuck, squabbles on the set, and back in the studio, the first *auteur* dying with most of the script in his head, the second quitting in disgust, and the last swearing it was finally in the can, but sneaking back to shoot some extra scenes.[6]

And with Michael Herr, who wrote:

In any other war, they would have made movies about us too, *Dateline: Hell!*, *Dispatch from Dong Ha*, maybe even *A Scrambler to the Front*, about Tim Page, Sean Flynn and Rick Merron, three young photographers who used to ride in and out of combat on Hondas. . . . So we have all been compelled to make our own movies, as many movies as there are correspondents, and this is mine. (One day at the battalion aid station in Hue a Marine with minor shrapnel wounds in his legs was waiting to get on a helicopter, a long wait with all of the dead and badly wounded going out first, and a couple of sniper rounds snapped across the airstrip, forcing us to move behind some sandbagging. "I hate this movie," he said, and I thought, "Why not?") My movie, my friends, my colleagues.[7]

The Stunt Man's portrayal of the Vietnam War as movie subtly represents the situation of the Vietnam veteran in American society of the eighties. In the film, elaborate, dangerous illusion and aimless post–Vietnam War reality contest

181

for a wandering Vietnam veteran's soul. In *The Stunt Man* that American dilemma is resolved comically, but on the set of *The Twilight Zone: The Movie* (1985), during the filming of scenes representing the Vietnam War, the black comedy of *The Stunt Man* turned into real tragedy with the deaths of actor Vic Morrow and two Vietnamese children. It was a striking case of life imitating art.

This whole series of comic book passes at the issues and themes of the Vietnam War focused almost exclusively on the theme of coming home and then somehow going back, either psychologically, as in *Some Kind of Hero* or *The Stunt Man* or *Cease Fire* (1986) or *Firefox* (1985), or actually (though unbelievably) physically returning to rescue those who were originally left behind, as in *The Deer Hunter*, *Uncommon Valor* (1983), *Rambo II*, and the *Missing in Action* (1984–87) films. This wishful survivor guilt fantasy best fit the comic book commando type and, culminating in *Rambo II* in 1986, was the essential plot of the majority of the films dealing with the legacy of Vietnam.

And then came 1987–88, the year of Vietnam at the movies, the second coming of 1977–78, when *Coming Home*, *The Deer Hunter*, and *Apocalypse Now* all appeared. In the short space of sixteen months, no less than six major Vietnam War films were released. Of these six, only *Platoon*, *Full Metal Jacket*, *Hamburger Hill*, and *Off Limits* are really about the Vietnam War. *Gardens of Stone* and *Good Morning Vietnam* are not really about the war itself. Of the six, *Full Metal Jacket* is the most important because it does what *Platoon* makes a valiant attempt to do. It gives full definition to the nihilism that all the soldiers in the Vietnam War films of the year feel. In John Del Vecchio's novel *The 13th Valley*, the recurring grunt expression of the nature of the infantryman's situation in Vietnam is "It don't mean nothin'." *Full Metal Jacket* also underscores that phrase and then, in a series of striking images, presents a full, highly symbolic view of that nihilistic approach to life in the Vietnam War. Thus, because the recurring conclusion that each film in its own way draws is that "It don't mean nothin'," Phase Three, the postmodernist phase of the history of the Vietnam War film, can be called the Symbolic Nihilist Phase.

What is important about this Symbolic Nihilist Phase of Vietnam War films is that, except for *Gardens of Stone*, all of the films are set in Vietnam, in the war. The consensus all of these films arrive at is that being in the Vietnam War occasioned an almost complete annihilation of a former, civilized, moral self, just as the circumstances of the war itself had accomplished a complete annihilation of the participant's

grasp of reality, morality, or sanity. As Conrad wrote in *Heart
of Darkness*, Vietnam was a world where everyone had been
"kicked loose of the earth" and was operating with "no re-
straint." Symbolic nihilism is the representation or dramati-
zation of an individual's or a group of individuals' gradual
movement into a void in which all positive aspects of the self,
all powers of self-determination and control of action and context are not simply temporarily lost, but rather are so totally
annihilated that the self no longer believes in any contexts,
no longer hopes for any progress toward any of the ideals,
moral designs, or social relationships that it held before entering that void. In literary/filmic terms, each of the major
Vietnam War films of 1987–88—*Platoon*, *Full Metal Jacket*,
Hamburger Hill, *Off Limits*—works on two levels of symbolic
interpretation. Each is a film of the initiation of the protag-
onists into nothingness, the annihilation of the self. Simultaneously, however, each is also a film about what Vietnam
did to America, how it annihilated the Kennedy idealism of
the early sixties, taking what had been the world's most powerful society's positive (even arrogant) sense of itself and humiliating that sense of itself into emptiness and complete
moral breakdown.

In *Going After Cacciato*, Paul Berlin's father tells him, "You'll
see some terrible stuff, I guess. That's how it goes. But try
to look for the good things, too. They'll be there if you look."
But for Chris Taylor in *Platoon*, for Joker in *Full Metal Jacket*,
for the whole faceless platoon in *Hamburger Hill*, and for the
two utterly confused cops in *Off Limits*, there are no good
things. They all realize, as did Sergeant Egan in *The 13th
Valley*, that "it don't mean nothin' " is ultimately the only
way that the nihilism of the Vietnam War can be encountered.
Those books and these films form a literature of rejection.
Their characters reject their former selves and realize that all
that is left for them is to wander like ghosts within the void
of those rejections.

Since the late seventies, parallel to the development of
these Vietnam War literary and film histories, there has been
a New Historicism afoot in American culture. Defined by
postmodernist theoreticians of history such as Hayden White
and Dominick LaCapra, it demands that history not only be
collected, ordered, and preserved, but that it also be read and
interpreted in all of its texts. This reading of history is not
restricted simply to the interpretation of historical events or
figures. Rather, it involves the reading of culture as a text in
all its multiplicity.

Oliver Stone, screenwriter and director of the films *Salva-
dor*, *Platoon*, *Wall Street*, and *Born on the Fourth of July*, wished

in a 1991 interview: "I'd like to be able to say, 'Hey, those films reflected a time and place that was pretty accurate. We caught a piece of Vietnam . . . a piece of the madness on Wall Street in the '80's. I'd like to leave that kind of legacy: That I was a good historian as well as a good dramatist.'"[8] That consciousness of the artist as historian creating a text for the time has, since 1977, been fully developed and read in the literary and film art dealing with the Vietnam War. Now, finally, here in Dennis Noble's collection of the visual art generated out of the Vietnam War, yet another version of that text of American cultural history is being offered. And one can read these works of visual art, either separately or together (as they are presented here), as a text, just as one can read Michael Herr's *Dispatches* or Stanley Kubrick's *Full Metal Jacket* as a historical and cultural text.

What is most striking about the collection of military art assembled herein is that these paintings can be read, in fact, demand to be read, both as individual texts and as a single, ordered historical text. As a historian, such as Stanley Karnow perhaps, presents not only a narrative of history but also the underlying themes and social statements of history, presents not only the sequence of events of a particular war in a particular time but also consciousness and feelings of the whole culture involved in that war, so too does a visual historian like Dennis Noble create a narrative and a cultural consciousness out of the arrangement and counterpoint and thematic connection of the paintings in this collection.

History functions on many different levels and finds form in many different sorts of texts. The visual history of the art of the Vietnam War is just such a text, and a hitherto unexplored one. Thanks to Dennis Noble that is no longer the case. His collection of the military art of the Vietnam War is a first step in curing that frustrating fragmentariness of images that Michael Herr writes about in the quotation that begins this essay. Noble's efforts are more a connection than a collection. They are a bringing together of those fragmented images of which Herr writes into a single text that we all can read.

NOTES

1. Michael Herr, *Dispatches* (New York: Alfred A. Knopf, 1977), 62–63.

2. Other major works of Vietnam War literature worth consulting are Stanley Karnow, *Vietnam: A History* (Penguin, 1984), Neil Sheehan, *The Bright Shining Lie* (Harper and Row, 1988), James Webb, *Fields of Fire* (Prentice-Hall, 1978), Gustav Hasford, *The Short Timers* (Harper and Row, 1979), Bobby Ann Mason, *Incountry* (Harper and Row, 1985), Donald Body,

F.N.G. (Viking, 1985), Philip Caputo, *Del Corso's Gallery* (Holt, Rinehart and Winston, 1983), and Truong Nhu Tang, *A Viet Cong Memoir* (Vintage, 1986).

3. In *Rethinking Intellectual History* (Ithaca, N.Y.: Cornell University Press, 1983), Dominick LaCapra writes:

> To refer to social or individual life as a text (or as "textualized") is in an obvious sense to employ a metaphor. But the metaphor is not a "mere" metaphor. It combines the polemical vehemence of assertion with the critical distance that counteracts dogmatism. The reliance on a metaphor to provide a way of seeing problems nonetheless involves linguistic inflation. If this risk comes with the opportunity to understand problems better than in alternative perspectives—for example, the one that takes "reality" or "context" as an unproblematic ground or gold standard—then the risk is well worth taking. But the metaphor of textuality is in no sense perfect, even as a medium for contesting the standard dichotomy between metaphor and its opposites (the literal, the conceptual, the serious, and so forth). (19)

4. Samuel Popkin, "A Sample Course and Its Rationale," paper delivered at the Conference on the Teaching of the Vietnam War, Washington, D.C., April 1988.

5. Greil Marcus, "Journey Up the River: An Interview with Francis Coppola," *Rolling Stone*, November 1, 1979.

6. Julian Smith, *Looking Away: Hollywood and Vietnam* (New York: Charles Scribner's Sons, 1975), 103.

7. Herr, *Dispatches*, 189.

8. *USA Weekend*, February 25, 1991.

SELECTED BIBLIOGRAPHY

Archival/Questionnaire

Correspondence Relating to War Artists of the AEF. Box 8, A.E.F., GHQ, G–2D, Record Group 120, National Archives Building, Washington, D.C.

Koczwara, Trella Chris. Completed questionnaire to Dennis L. Noble, October 31, 1990.

Military Art Collections

U.S. Air Force Art Collection, The Pentagon.

U.S. Army Art Collection, Center of Military History, Alexandria, Va.

U.S. Coast Guard Art Collection, U.S. Coast Guard Headquarters, Washington, D.C.

U.S. Marine Corps Historical Center, Washington Navy Yard, Washington, D.C.

U.S. Navy Combat Art Collection, Washington Navy Yard, Washington, D.C.

Books on War and Art

Antone, Evan Haywood. *Tom Lea, His Life and Work*, El Paso: Texas Western Press, 1988.

Anzenberger, Joseph F., Jr., ed. *Combat Art of the Vietnam War.* Jefferson, N.C.: McFarland and Co., 1986.

Brodie, Howard. *War Drawings: World War II and Korea.* Palo Alto, Calif.: National Press, 1962.

Crane, Aimee. *Art in the Armed Forces: Pictured by Men in Action.* New York: Hyperion Press, 1944.

Eby, Kerr. *War.* New Haven: Yale University Press, 1936.

Fischer, Katrina Sigsbee. *Anton Otto Fischer, Marine Artist.* Nantucket, Mass.: Mill Hill Press, 1984.

Fox, Milton S. *The Use of Art and Artists in Times of War. A Summary of a Detailed and Documented Study Written February 1941.* Cleveland: Cleveland Museum of Art, 1942.

German War Art. New York: Crescent Books, 1983.

Henri, Raymond. *Vietnam Combat Art*. New York: Cavanagh and Cavanagh, 1968.

Hjerter, Kathleen G. *The Art of Tom Lea*. College Station: Texas A&M University Press, 1989.

Hodgson, Pat. *The War Illustrators*. New York: Macmillan, 1977.

Jamieson, Mitchell. *Two Wars*. Washington, D.C.: The Gallery, 1979.

Johnson, Peter. *Front Line Artists*. London: Cassell, 1978.

Jones, James. *WW II*. New York: Grossett and Dunlap, 1975.

Karolevitz, Robert F. *The Prairie Is My Garden*. Aberdeen, S.D.: North Plains Press, 1969.

———. *Where Your Heart Is*. Aberdeen, S.D.: North Plains Press, 1970.

Kennedy Gallery. *Art of the Civil and Spanish American Wars, October 2 to November 10, 1980*. New York: Kennedy Gallery, 1980.

Lea, Tom. *Battle Stations*. Dallas: Still Point Press, 1988.

Library of Congress. *Artists for Victory*. Washington, D.C.: Library of Congress, 1983.

Lippard, Lucy R. *A Different Kind of War: Vietnam in Art*. Seattle: Real Comet Press, 1990.

Okamoto, Shumpei. *Impressions of the Front*. Philadelphia: Philadelphia Museum of Art, 1983.

Reep, Edward. *A Combat Artist in World War II*. Lexington: University Press of Kentucky, 1987.

Thomas, Denis. *Arms and the Artist*. Oxford: Phardon Press, 1977.

25th Infantry Division. *Combat Art of the 25th Infantry "Tropic Lightning" Division*. Vol. 1. Tokyo: Tosho Printing Co., 1967.

Tyler, Ronnie C. *The Mexican War*. Austin: Texas State Historical Association, 1973.

United States. Army Service Force. Special Services Division. *Soldier Art*. Washington, D.C.: Infantry Journal, 1945.

Waterhouse, Charles. *Vietnam Sketchbook: Drawings from Delta to DMZ*. Rutland, Vt.: Charles E. Tuttle, 1968.

———. *Vietnam War Sketches: From the Air, Land, and Sea*. Rutland, Vt.: Charles E. Tuttle, 1970.

Weber, John Paul. *The German War Artists*. Columbia, S.C.: Cerberus Book Co., 1979.

Books on the Vietnam War

Anderson, Kent. *Sympathy for the Devil*. Garden City, N.Y.: Doubleday, 1987.

Baker, Mark. *Nam: The Vietnam War in the Words of the Men and Women Who Fought There*. New York: Quill, 1982.

Bunting, Josiah. *The Lionheads*. New York: Popular Library, 1972.

Cash, John A., John Albright, and Allen W. Sandstrum. *Seven Firefights in Vietnam*. Washington, D.C.: Office of the Chief of Military History, U.S. Army, 1970.

Croizat, Victor. *The Brown Water Navy: The River and Coastal War in Indo-China and Vietnam, 1948–1972*. Dorset, England: Blandford Press, 1984.

Cutler, Thomas J. *Brown Water, Black Berets: Coastal and Riverine Warfare in Vietnam*. Annapolis, Md.: Naval Institute Press, 1988.

Davis, Larry. *Gunships: A Pictorial History of Spooky*. Carrollton, Tex.: Squadron/Signal Publications, 1982.

Doleman, Edgar C., Jr., and the editors of Boston Publishing Company. *Tools of War*. Boston: Boston Publishing Co., 1984.

Dougan, Clark, Stephen Wise, and the editors of Boston Publishing Company. *The American Experience in Vietnam*. New York: W. W. Norton, 1988.

Duncan, David Douglas. *This Is War! A Photo-Narrative in Three Parts*. New York: Harper and Brothers, 1951.

———. *War Without Heroes*. New York: Harper, 1970.

Edelman, Bernard, ed. *Dear America: Letters Home from Vietnam*. New York: Bantam Books, 1985.

Ethell, Jeffrey, and Alfred Price. *One Day in a Long Air War: May 10, 1972 Air War, North Vietnam*. New York: Random House, 1989.

Fall, Bernard, *Street Without Joy*. New York: Schocken Books, 1972.

Fitzgerald, Frances. *Fire in the Lake: The Vietnamese and the Americans in Vietnam*. Boston: Little, Brown, 1972.

Fulton, William B. *Riverine Operations, 1966–1969*. Washington, D.C.: Government Printing Office, 1973.

Hammel, Eric M. *Khe Sanh: Siege in the Clouds. An Oral History*. New York: Crown, 1989.

Herr, Michael. *Dispatches*. New York: Alfred A. Knopf, 1977.

Karnow, Stanley. *Vietnam: A History*. New York: Viking, 1983.

Kimler, Forest L., ed. *Boondock Bards*. San Francisco: Stars and Stripes, 1968.

Larteguy, Jean. *The Centurions*. New York: E. P. Dutton, 1962.

Morrocco, John. *Rain of Fire: Air War, 1969–1973*. Boston: Boston Publishing Co., 1985.

———. *Thunder from Above: Air War, 1941–1968*. Boston: Boston Publishing Co., 1984.

Nalty, Bernard C. *Air Power and the Fight for Khe Sanh*. Washington, D.C.: Office of Air Force History, U.S. Air Force, 1973.

Oberdorfer, Don. *Tet!* Garden City, N.Y.: Doubleday, 1971.

O'Brien, Tim. *Going After Cacciato*. New York: Delacorte Press, 1978.

Peterson, Michael E. *The Combined Action Platoons: The U.S. Marines' Other War in Vietnam*. New York: Praeger, 1989.

Pisnor, Robert. *The End of the Line: The Siege of Khe Sanh*. New York: W. W. Norton, 1982.

Roth, Robert. *Sand in the Wind*. Boston: Little, Brown, 1971.

Santoli, Al. *Everything We Had: An Oral History of the Vietnam War by Thirty-Three American Soldiers Who Fought It*. New York: Random House, 1981.

Simpson, Charles M. III. *Inside the Green Berets: The First Thirty Years. A History of the U.S. Army Special Forces*. Novato, Calif.: Presidio Press, 1983.

Telfer, Gary L., Lane Rogers, and V. Keith Flemming, Jr. *U.S. Marines in Vietnam: Fighting the North Vietnamese, 1967*. Washington, D.C.: U.S. Marine Corps, 1984.

Tulich, Eugene N. *The United States Coast Guard in South East Asia During the Vietnam Conflict*. Washington, D.C.: U.S. Coast Guard, Public Affairs Division, 1975.

U.S. Congress. Senate. *Medal of Honor Recipients, 1863–1978*. Committee on Veterans' Affairs, Senate Committee Print No. 3, 96th Congress, 1st Session, February 14, 1979.

U.S. Marine Corps. *The Marines in Vietnam, 1954–1973: An Anthology and Annotated Bibliography*. Washington, D.C.: U.S. Marine Corps, 1974. Reprinted 1983.

West, Francis J., Jr. *Small Unit Action in Vietnam, Summer 1966.* Washington, D.C.: Historical Branch, U.S. Marine Corps, 1967.

Westmoreland, William C. *A Soldier Reports.* Garden City, N.Y.: Doubleday, 1976.

Articles on Art

Heinz, W. C. "Sketching John Groth." *50 Plus* 26, no. 11 (November 1986): 42–48.

Howell, Edgar M. "An Artist Goes to War: Harvey Dunn and the A.E.F. War Art Program." *Smithsonian Journal of History* 2, no. 4 (Winter 1967–1968): 45–56.

Kemp, John R. "Henry Casselli." *American Artist* 51 (August 1987): 48–53, 85–87.

Mangan, Doreen. "Henry Casselli: Superb Contradictions." *American Artist* 38 (December 1974): 39–43.

Sandoz, Mari. "The Look of the Last Frontier." *American Heritage* 12, no. 4 (June 1961): 42–53.

White, Bill. "Lady Combat Artist." *Leatherneck* 71, no. 6 (June 1987): 40–45.

Articles on the Vietnam War

Hodgman, James A. "Market Time in the Gulf of Thailand." *Naval Review* (1968): 36–67.

Miller, Richards T. "Fighting Boats of the United States." *Naval Review* (1968): 297–329.

Noble, Dennis L. "Cutters and Sampans." U.S. Naval Institute *Proceedings* 110 (June 1984): 46–53.

Palm, Edward F. "Tiger Papa Three: A Memoir of the Combined Action Program, Part I." *Marine Corps Gazette* (January 1988): 34–43.

———. "Tiger Papa Three: The Fire Next Time, Part Two." *Marine Corps Gazette* (February 1988): 66–76.

Schreadley, Richard L. "The Naval War in Vietnam, 1950–1970." U.S. Naval Institute *Proceedings* 97 (May 1971): 180–209.

———. "Swift Raiders." U.S. Naval Institute *Proceedings* 110 (June 1984): 53–56.

Summers, Harry G., Jr. "The Bitter Triumph of Ia Drang." *American Heritage* 35, no. 2 (February/March 1984): 50–59.

Toplin, Robert Brent. "Television's Civil War." *Perspectives: American Historical Association Newsletter* 28, no. 6 (September 1990): 1, 22, 24.

INDEX TO ART
(by Location)

U.S. Air Force Art Collection

The Pentagon

U.S. Army Art Collection

Center of Military History, Alexandria, Va.

U.S. Coast Guard Art Collection

U.S. Coast Guard Headquarters, Washington, D.C.

U.S. Marine Corps Art Collection

U.S. Marine Corps Historical Center Washington Navy Yard, Washington, D.C.

U.S. Navy Combat Art Collection

Washington Navy Yard, Washington, D.C.

GENERAL INDEX

About the Author

DENNIS L. NOBLE has devoted his life and career to the military and its history. Retired from the U.S. Coast Guard in 1978, Dr. Noble is the author of several military history books. He manages the Washington State Library Branch at the Clallam Bay Corrections Center and teaches at Peninsula College in Port Angeles, Washington. He is the author of *The Eagle and the Dragon: The U.S. Military in China, 1901–1937* (Greenwood Press, 1990).